MASS PERSUASION METHOD

Activate the 8 psychological switches that make people open their hearts, minds and wallets for you (without knowing why they are doing it)

BUSHRA AZHAR

Founder of The Persuasion Revolution

"Where Tiny Businesses Make Big Bucks Using the Psychology of Persuasion" www.ThePersuasionRevolution.com

To Aun & Ayzah. The relentless master
persuaders of our household

To Nado. I carry your heart with me,
I carry you in my heart

TABLE OF CONTENTS

PREFACE

Before we start, I ask that you brave a series of unfortunate disclaimers:

If you consider undergarments to be "unmentionables" or you are fundamentally opposed to using the F-word as a conversation enhancer, stop reading right now.

If references to bodily fluids offend you, this book is decidedly not for you. I happen to pride myself on using bodily fluids as nouns, pronouns, verbs, adverbs *and* adjectives.

If you made it past those first three disclaimers a-okay, then I'm obligated to issue another warning:

This is no ordinary book.

I know, I know... Everyone and their dad say that about their books... Even if their books are worth less than the paper they're printed on and have little use outside of recycling said paper to wipe one's bum.

Here's why I am confident you will prevent this copy of *Mass Persuasion Method* from suffering such a fate:

By the time your eyes read the final sentence on the last page of this book, you will have acquired the super-power of persuasion that allows you to…

- Get your spouse to do the dishes with a smile (a tall order I know)

- Inspire your customers to practically fight over each other to hand you their money and get ahold of whatever you're selling

- Influence experts, authorities and relevant leaders in your field to send more opportunities your way than you could have ever accessed on your own

- Possibly attract a stalker or two because you have made yourself SO irresistible to regular folks who haven't made the hooray-worthy life choice of buying this book

This, I can guarantee — you will have such a grasp of ethical, works-in-all-contexts persuasion that you can convince me to drop my Nutella-covered croissant and pick up a plain kale salad.

On your way to mastering the art and understanding the science of persuasion, you will come face-to-page with trolls, flustered chickens and red-hot mama's and papa's.

And you'll realize it was well worth the adventure — because your mastery and understanding of persuasion will manifest in an almost supernatural ability to inspire incredible loyalty and forge lifelong bonds and honest connections with your tribe of online followers and fans.

The ultimate result?

You'll understand how to hook, pull, draw, magnetize and altogether mesmerize your customers and potential customers into buying from you, above everyone else in your industry...and more than once!

Mass Persuasion Method is the secret code that – once unlocked – motivates people to:

- Open their wallets and drops their email addresses and send you love notes...Even if you don't have foxy glamour shots of yourself smiling coyly at them with a "Come Hither" look.

- Tell their friends, family, doctor, neighbors, in-law's... everyone about you!

- ...And when they are done with that? They will whisper your website address to their pets (because that is how much they love you).

HOW TO USE THIS BOOK

Most of the time, assuming ANY thing about someone is a mistake.

Lo and behold, this is *not* one of those times.

Because now that you're reading this book, I can assume that at least one thing about you is true:

The phrases *"If only I had more time…"*, *"I just can't…No time"* or a more Garfield-y *"So much to do, so little time!"* have become your go-to descriptions of your life, your schedule and how little time there is to get it all done.

As for that oh-so desirable miracle called "free time," you can either occupy said time eating/sleeping/pooping or you can attend a 90-minute webinar that gives you the magic formula to make you 20 years younger, 10 points smarter and possibly restore your virginity.

But how's a body ever supposed to do both?

"I just can't…No time!"

I get it…I really do.

There are more days than I'd like to admit where I've held my pee for HOURS just so I can reply to the next email…and the next one, and the next one…

Don't pretend to be shocked. You've done the same, I bet. *Because hey, you're a super busy entrepreneur!*

Your to-do list stretches from here to the next continent… and back.

Who wants to read a 1,000-page monstrosity that makes you want to scream after it meanders along for 400 pages and takes 'til around page 867 to get to the damn point?

That's why this little book is written with you in mind — or more specifically, that unspoken "Do Not Waste My Time Or I Will Cut You" policy most of us wish we could implement.

That's why I kept this book as short as I could. The content is laid out so it's all **easy to read** and **easy to implement**. It shouldn't take you more than a few hours (if that) to get through it.

You'll also find throughout these pages real-life success stories of entrepreneurs and business owners like you who are tickled hot-pink by the results they are seeing because they implemented *Mass Persuasion Method.*

All praise in these **The Proof Is In The Persuasion** mini sections comes to you completely uncensored of course!

THE PROOF IS IN THE PERSUASION:

Satya Kothimangalam
Yesterday at 8:52am

I created a Landing Page for a client using MPM and its converting at over 30%. He has never seen numbers this high and is over the moon! Yeeha - thanks Bushra for everything!

👍 Like   💬 Comment

To introduce you to every persuasion strategy, tactic, tip and twerk (*really, Bushra?*) that work to transform your business into a persuasion powerhouse too, *Mass Persuasion Method* is divided into 4 Segments:

Segment 1: Harness the Power Of Persuasion

Right from the get-go, discover the missing piece you need to become the next phenomenal online Success Story worth sharing a few thousand times on social media...

You know, the kind of success that makes everyone around you feel like shit!

Just joking...don't do that. Be nice.

The ability to persuade on demand, on command is the single most important factor for selling your products or services online.

Knowing the *Why* and mastering the *How* of effective, sleaze-free persuasion can transform your business from one that's limping along or producing *negative* Return-On-Investment (not good)...

...to one that rockets past the hapless competition to the top of your industry, with jingling bells dangling happily from the tail!

Side Note: Do rockets have tails?

Segment 2: Mass Persuasion Method In Action

Yours truly will show you how to mesmerize the masses without removing a single item of clothing!

It's time to combine your newly developed persuasion proficiency with the limitless reach of the internet to gain loyal (and rabid) fans who love you and drool over whatever you put out there that has a Buy Now button.

Because nobody wants theory, you'll get practical, straight-from-my-six-figure-launches secrets for creating memorable videos (and have fun doing it).

Then you'll follow a proven, generic advice-free path to become a (non-annoying) social media star on Facebook — so that every post gets liked, commented and shared by the masses.

And finally on to home base (gutter much?) where you'll craft emails that are SO good, people actually read the entire message AND look forward to seeing your name in their inbox! No small miracle right there.

Segment 3: Your Super-Persuasive No-Defying, Cash-Pumping Offer

Business is about selling.

Things.

Ideas.

YOU.

No, not *that* way, you gutterbrain.

No sale happens unless money exchanges hands.

And no money exchanges hands unless there is an offer.

But before we work our way through the nuts and bolts of your compelling offer, you need to know exactly what makes people utter the most dreaded word in the English language in response to your pitch…

The DREADED "NO".

Knowing what makes people say NO is the first step to getting them to say YES.

Once you know those reasons better than your own customers do – thanks to *Mass Persuasion Method* – we can design an offer for your product or service that gets an easy YES!

In Segment 3, you will find a step by step breakdown of all the elements that go into your offer — plus a look at the different types of offers to create.

That way, you will always be sure your customers are happy, satisfied and ready to recommend you to their stylist, their dog trainer and their dog trainer's grandmother.

Segment 4: Persuasion Quickies

Consider this Segment a *How-to-Persuade-in-Real-Life* bonus! Because most books in the online business genre give you a whole lot of "what" with only few measly hints as to the "how," I believe you deserve better.

There's no worse feeling than purchasing "advice", only to feel more confused than you did before you bought the damn thing!

This Segment equips you with *do-this-then-that* tactics that will feel like a swift kick in the behind to take your newfound persuasive powers out into the world (and straight into your business).

To that end, you'll see how to infuse the most YES-inducing elements of persuasion in a pitch to your potential customers when you're on a live call or when you speak to them face to face.

No sleaze here — just a clean, clear and credible connection with your buyers so they come to know, love and trust you in minutes (not months or years).

You'll also find Quickie Persuasion Boosters that you MUST include in your copywriting so that your words jump off the page and grab your readers by the throat (not to strangle them but pull them in oh-so lovingly).

Once you Quickie Boost your copy, your audience of potential customers won't be able to stop reading your website, your sales page, your webinar landing page, your promotional emails and all the rest.

Nutella-Covered Nuggets O' Wisdom

A list of "Nutella-Covered Nuggets O' Wisdom" follows each and every Chapter — a speedy recap of the key points, highlights and unforgettables.

Consider these sweet, ambrosial treats a quick overview of the chapter you just read (and a brain-gasm because Nutella will be stuck in your head, minus the calories).

Thanks to these Nuggets, once you check this book off your reading list you can come back to scan again and again to be reminded where it all began — the fundamentals of effective, non-icky persuasion that work wherever and whenever you apply them.

They may also work if you are craving something sweet — probably not, but no harm in trying, right?

I recommend that you read *Mass Persuasion Method* all the way through the first time, then hone in on the chapters most relevant for the next stage of your business' growth.

Whatever happens, don't feel like you need to start implementing ALL of these ideas the minute you discover them.

So read cover to cover.

Understand the strategy.

Absorb the tactics.

See which ones most align with your brand and personality.

Then get ready to implement.

And get ready to be blown away because…

Persuasion works like bloody magic.

You'll knock your customers' socks off.

They'll fall truly, madly, deeply in love with you, your ideas and everything you sell them.

You'll have them turning cartwheels, dancing in the streets and erecting monuments in your honor.

And you're going to love every minute of this madness.

Welcome to Mass Persuasion Method.

INTRODUCTION

Most nonfiction books begin with a drier-as-my-cuticles explanation of everything that follows the Introduction chapter.

Although many a sand dune can be found on my hands, you can probably tell already that my book isn't like most.

So, no unnecessary previews here. Instead, I want to share with you my *re*-definition of persuasion and why I maintain the stance that persuasion is not icky, manipulative or used Car salesman-esque like most people assume it is.

Persuasion isn't something one person does to the other. It is what one person does to herself as an internal response to the stimulus she is exposed to.

Her personal ticks that respond favorably to the stimulus — these are what cause her to be persuaded...

...not some sleazy dark magic but she HERSELF!

So **when you know** what makes her tick...

And **when you know** what's going on in her brain as she reads your copy, your emails, your sales page...

And **when you know** how to get into her heart, mind and yes her wallet (10 points for those of you who thought I was going to say pants!)…

You will get her to buy from you even if your site looks like an overzealous 2 year old attacked it with a bunch of broken crayons and a free WordPress template.

You will get her to surrender her credit card even if you *don't* look like you just strolled out of a Victoria's Secret photo shoot.

And you will get her to pay attention to you and hang on every last word you say even if she's never heard of you before.

How do I know this? Because all of the above is true about me.

I had a website that looked like something the cat threw up.

I certainly don't look like a Victoria's Secret model, and when I was first starting out, no one in my target market had ever heard of me.

I'm sharing all of this for **just one reason**:

I want you to know in your heart and in your bones that if I can do it, **so can you**.

Shout that from the rooftops!

Hire one of those sky-writing biplanes!

Engrave it on your forehead!

Tattoo it to your butt!

I did all of this without special friends in high places, without an audience already in place to launch products to and without a ton of play money to throw at my business.

I did this without being part of 5 different masterminds, attending 8 different networking events or hiring 3 high level mindset coaches.

This all means that you too can achieve unbelievable success in your online business without any of the things you "have to have" (according to the experts).

No pretty website.

No mastermind groups.

No coach.

No connections.

You don't even have to live on the same side of the world as your customers do.

Or speak the same language they do (non-native English speaker here, selling to native speakers).

I was (and still am) living in a time zone that is disruptively different than just about 95% of my customers.

And still I manage to draw in more and more people to buy my online programs.

My tribe keeps expanding.

My list keeps growing.

My impact keeps spreading.

My income keeps escalating.

And my head keeps spinning with all the crazy, wonderful, fantastic things I get to experience.

All in under two years.

And all because I knew how to work with the beautiful, magical, amazing, gorgeous, powerful thing called persuasion.

And now you can, too.

Ready to persuade?

SEGMENT 1

HARNESS THE POWER OF PERSUASION

CHAPTER 1

WHY PERSUADE?

Persuasion is everywhere.

No matter where you look and no matter who you're dealing with, you're either trying to persuade someone or someone is trying to persuade you.

Think about this for a moment:

In every conversation, interaction or connection, you are either the "persuade-e" or the "persuade-r."

If you don't persuade your boss to your view – that you deserve a raise or promotion – she will persuade **you** that you're not ready for that raise.

And you'll walk out of there *believing* you need to work for another year (or 10) before you'll be considered for a promotion... or even deserve one. Ouch.

With something so powerful at your fingertips and tongue tip (aka persuasion), you as an entrepreneur must become not just so-so at persuading the masses...

You must become a Master Persuader.

How else are people going to choose to buy from you?

How else are you going to create customers?

Because **your business is only as successful as the number of customers you manage to persuade.**

And not just persuade *once*, but over and over...and over.

And what are you trying to persuade them to do?

Say, "Yes!"

That's it.

If you get them to say yes, you're in business. . .and you *stay* in business.

The more and more people who start saying yes to you, the more successful – and I mean **super successful** – you become.

Yes to you, your ideas and your work.

Yes to your product or service.

Yes to your program or offer.

And of course, yes to your price — and to paying you.

I'm talking an *avalanche* of yeses. Stand back and watch that money pour into your account!

I can already hear you saying, "So, how do I get potential customers to say yes?"

Glad you asked, my darling buttercup.

Because I'm going to tell you how to:

OUT-SHINE, OUT-SELL, OUT-MASTER

Here's the good news...

Most people, especially your competitors, are absolutely clueless when it comes to persuasion. If you improve your skill by just 2%, you can *out-shine*, *out-sell* and *out-master* everyone in your industry.

That is precisely what I teach through The Persuasion Revolution – and through the book you're reading now.

So here's the better news...

You don't have to work like a lunatic, pouring over hefty books and medical journals, cramming information till your brain is about to explode.

How do you out-shine, out-sell and out-master the competition without hustling like a madwoman 20 hours a day?

Improve your persuasion skills by just 2%.

That's it. You're in business.

The business of persuading people to part with their cash in exchange for your brilliance — whether that is your service, product, program or offering...

Or yourself!

The more you practice, the more you flex those persuasion muscles in every piece of copy and every page of your website and every post on social media...

The better you get at the thing that creates new customers — *persuasion.*

This isn't rocket science.

It's neuroscience.

But not the type of science that forces you to don a lab coat-and-goggles outfit to study.

To grow your business into a persuasion powerhouse, start by imagining the human brain as an electrical circuit.

90% of purchasing decisions in the buyer's mind are the result of someone sparking that circuit into action.

We *think* we make purchasing decisions by following a rational approach, carefully and methodically weighing the pros and cons.

But that's not how persuasion works. A "good" product doesn't sell itself.

Persuasion by design happens when you manage to make people feel something.

When you evoke desire for your thing.

When you demolish all the objections, cynicism and disbelief even the most jaded buyer has.

The result?

People stop scrolling and start drooling.

People scramble for their credit cards.

People take to their social media soapboxes on your behalf, telling the world how much they love you.

Hell, yeah!

And the best part about this excuse-disarming, desire-cultivating, wallet-opening thing called persuasion is that **you don't have to be a natural at persuasion, to persuade!**

One more time for the skimmers among us:

You don't have to be a natural at persuasion, to persuade!

I created The Persuasion Revolution because the "poo-rus" would have you believe that the ability to convince others to buy your shit comes naturally to only a tiny, tiny exclusive group of people (them).

What hope does that leave for the rest of us?

THE PROOF IS IN THE PERSUASION:

Shannon Dahlen
March 22 at 12:24am · North Richland Hills, TX, United States

In the last two years (more like 18 months but whatever), I have spent right around 40K on business programs, coaching, shiny objects - all kinds of shit I don't need. After going through the info in MPM, Ph Lab, and EPS, you know what I realized? I could have saved myself 38.5K because Bushra teaches you everything you need to know -And she does it better than any of the programs I've taken so far.

The unfortunate result of this belief – which most aspiring online entrepreneurs have – is that the most critical aspect of their businesses gets outsourced to copywriters, strategists and designers.

"But I'm not good at persuading people!"

29

I would take a good clean bet that this thought has planted itself inside your cranium at some point in your life before picking up (or downloading) this book.

Here's where I'm about to make your life a living *heaven*.

If you do anything online, you need to understand what makes people tick.

Not your copywriter.

Not your strategist.

Not your designer.

You.

Or you will continue face-planting the wall of no. This is not what I want for you.

That's why the entire premise of Mass Persuasion Method is to treat the human brain like an electrical circuit with 8 "Persuasion Switches."

Activate all 8 through your messaging, and people will do what you want them to do.

Flip the Persuasion Switches in the human brain, and the brain of your buyer says YES.

See? Persuading someone doesn't require you to master the textbooks or manifest the people skills of Oprah!

Since we humans don't live all of our lives online (OK maybe I'm the exception…almost), the 8 Persuasion Switches work in offline business and in your daily one-on-one interactions with people as well.

I have used the Persuasion Switches to get discounts and to upgrade to business class flight when I, at the time, could not afford business class.

I have used the Persuasion Switches to skip ahead in queues, which a lot of people would frown on.

But when you have two kids under five years old and they are constantly trying to force their way back into the birth canal, you better start flipping Switches to get to the front of that queue. Trust me on this.

The idea isn't to manipulate people or make them do what you want them to in a sleazy, iffy way.

If you can expose people to a certain stimulus – an advertisement, sales page, webinar pitch, optin page etc. – where you share something that makes them more prone to saying yes to you…

That is *ethical* persuasion done right.

Seriously, if you want your business to grow like a weed – a beautiful, enviable, cash-blooming weed – then you want persuasion on your side.

THE PROOF IS IN THE PERSUASION:

 Stephanie
15 hrs

Bushra!!!!

First webinar tonight; 13 viewed it (tiny tiny number) just sent out the link to sales page and I have my first sale!

Is it normal to feel so emotional after your first launch haha!!!

Thank you, thank you, thank you. X

In the next chapter, you'll become a Persuasionista by studying all 8 Persuasion Switches (and how to activate them in your future buyers' brains so they happily whip out their credit cards).

Ready to flip some Switches (and make bank)?

Nutella-Covered Nuggets O' Wisdom

You are either the "persuade-r" or the "persuade-e" in every conversation and interaction. There is no in-between.

To build a successful business online or off, you need to get lots of customers saying "yes" to your products and services. Getting to that yes is just a matter of understanding what makes them tick.

The human brain is basically a circuit. If you want to spark that circuit into taking the desired action, you have to activate the 8 Persuasion Switches first.

CHAPTER 2

THE 8 PERSUASION SWITCHES

This is it.

Welcome to the fundamental framework that's going to take you from so-so revenue (or a forehead-meets-keyboard failing business) to yeah, baby, I'm a rock-star entrepreneur and I'm singing all the way to the bank!

The quick backstory on these oh-so profitable Switches:

I developed the framework for the 8 Persuasion Switches during my past life as a business consultant.

At that time, I called it The Client Persuasion Framework (boring, I know).

But because this framework secured contracts ranging from several hundred thousand dollars up into the millions…

I knew the content was solid — that name just needed some jazzing up!

The 8 Persuasion Switches work through your communication, your content and your copy to apply every persuasion principle needed to make a sale.

In short, flip the Switches, make the sale — it's that simple.

Not only that, but Persuasion Switch-flipping comes with the added bonus that customers feel *happy* about buying from you.

Thanks to the 8 Persuasion Switches, you get to sidestep that terrible "troll under the bridge" that jumps out without warning and gobbles up your chances of making a sale.

The troll has a name: **Buyer's Remorse**.

Buyer's Remorse strikes when someone purchases your product or service, then instantly feels remorse and regret about clicking that Buy Button.

Another reason you want that troll to hibernate under that bridge for eternity:

Buyer's Remorse leads its victims to a destination all entrepreneurs hate, one called **Refund City**.

The last thing you need as a super-busy entrepreneur is to be forced to deal with refund requests by the truckload.

Luckily, you are investing your brain cells in learning the 8 Persuasion Switches, using them in your business, avoiding Buyer's Remorse and keeping refunds at a minimum.

Buckle up, grab your tea and meet the first Persuasion Switch you will flip like a MOFO in everything you do online (and off).

PERSUASION SWITCH #1
THE PRESTIGE SWITCH

The Prestige Switch is all about status — but not necessarily *your* status (put that ego to bed!).

When you flip the Prestige Switch in your copy and in conversations with potential buyers, you reveal how your product or service will elevate *their* status.

It's not quite as simple as saying, "If you buy this, you'll elevate your status and become rich and everyone will love you!"

If only, right?

That's because this Switch has 2 key dimensions that are worth tattooing next to your new bum art from the Introduction:

- Prestige Boosters
- Prestige Diminishers

Prestige Boosters are the objects, traits or experiences that the Everday Joe or Joanna thinks will level-up their personal or professional status in their own network, their industry and society as a whole.

Prestige Boosters include:

- literal wealth (AKA moolah)
- physical beauty
- charming personality
- influence over others' opinions
- being in the "inner circle"
- knowing something important or useful that others don't

Your buyers need to BELIEVE you will help them improve their status through as many Prestige Boosters as possible that are relevant to your offer.

Now, here's the tricky bit...

Prestige Boosters work best in your sales copy and messaging when potential buyers feel confident that making a purchasing won't *diminish* their current status.

In other words, *gain without the pain...the "yay" without the "boo"*.

This is where Prestige Diminishers require your acknowledgement.

No matter what you say or what you sell, make it crystal clear that your offer will help buyers escape these Diminishers.

The Prestige Diminishers include:

- shame from making a poor choice
- fear of being taken advantage of
- poverty
- physical unattractiveness
- being out of the loop

To Turn On The Prestige Switch, Make Sure Your Copy And Messaging Answer These Questions:

(i) Does my offer contain at least 2-3 Prestige Boosters?

(ii) Does my supporting copy address (and destroy) 1 or more Prestige Diminishers?

The Prestige Switch At Work: An Example

Win over the heart of your dream woman without worrying about being rejected or insulted in front of all your friends.

How the Prestige Booster implies higher social status:

Win over the heart of your dream woman...

How the Prestige Diminisher promises that public shame is not something to worry about:

...without worrying about being rejected or insulted in front of all your friends.

Swipe This Switch:

- Use this Switch in your optin offer or sales page headline to reel in your audience hook, line and sinker.

- Include a Prestige Booster in your business' or products' value proposition(s).

- Annihilate Prestige Diminishers in your supporting copy using vivid, sensory "feel like I'm actually there" language to cultivate an emotional response.

- Show potential customers how they can achieve the results they're craving WITHOUT suffering the roadblocks they're currently facing (or worry they will face and have no solution for).

PERSUASION SWITCH #2
THE BELIEVABILITY SWITCH

If you have heard the sales gurus or read the business books that tell you to focus on making your customers believe – and stay convinced – that your product or service will get them the results they want...

...you only got half the story.

Because getting your customers to believe in *themselves* and their OWN ability to achieve the desired results — this is where the battle for the sale is won.

Like the Prestige Switch, the Believability Switch has 2 dimensions — both of which cement, re-inforce and maintain:

- Their belief in you, your ideas, and your products or services
- Their belief in themselves — that *they* have what it takes to experience the results they desire by purchasing and using your products or services

If you only present one of these dimensions in your copy or messaging, the Switch won't flip.

Your sales message will fall flat on its face.

And they won't believe you.

To Turn On The Believability Switch, Ensure That Your Copy Answers These Questions:

(i) Does my product or service description include the phrase "so that" to describe *how* my offer will help them achieve their desired results?

(ii) Does my copy motivate the potential customer to believe in the product's ability to get them results *and* their own ability to achieve those results — AKA "I can do this"?

The Believability Switch At Work: An Example

This sports bra is made with the finest breathable fabric so that your boobs don't suffocate to death while you create your new body. It allows you to move with ease so you'll be able to work

38

out in comfort for hours, even if it's your first time at the gym.

How the key feature takes advantage of the "so that" extension:

This sports bra is made with the finest breathable fabric so that your boobs

don't suffocate to death while you create your new body...

How potential customers are inspired to believe in the product and in their ability to use it properly:

...It allows you to move with ease so you'll be able to work out in comfort for hours, even if it's your first time at the gym.

Swipe This Switch:

Describe your proven, step-by step roadmap or framework that has helped others get results.

Use this mini template when describing features to minimize the fear that it won't work out as hoped: *"This [FEATURE] is [WHY IT'S SO GREAT] so that you don't suffer [BURNING PAIN POINT]".*

Position yourself as the premier subject matter expert by offering proof you have achieved the results they want, too — *and* how you have helped others just like them achieve those results.

Show your customer they owe it to themselves to benefit from your solution and stop wasting time and energy on sub-par products that over-promise and under-deliver.

Use non-generic, results-focused testimonials from previous buyers that pinpoint precisely how your product or service changed their lives or businesses forever.

PERSUASION SWITCH #3
THE PARITY SWITCH

The entrepreneur who understands their buyers' objections is the entrepreneur who can make their products or services sell like Nutella-drenched hotcakes.

After all, with SO many different products and services available in your industry, how else are you going to convince your market to give *you* their hard-earned moolah?

By flipping the Parity Switch, you are using your buyers' objections *in your favor* to position you and your offer as the very best solution to their unsolved problem or unachieved goal.

A Side Note From Bushra:

The Parity Switch isn't just about positioning yourself to appear "better" than the competition.

Because the competition doesn't end with other businesses in your industry or area of expertise.

No ma'am (or sir)! There's another alternative that is much harder to out-compete:

Your customers themselves.

Your biggest competitor isn't an entrepreneur in your niche who has endorsements from Oprah, Dr. Oz or Forbes…

…it's your own customer's lack of "get up and go"!

If your customer is not absolutely convinced that you and your product or service is **a safer, better alternative to doing nothing** (or just hoping things change on their own), you have officially lost the sale.

The solution is to strategically populate your copy and messaging with proof that the greater risk to them, the customers, is *not* buying from you!

The resulting thought in your buyers' minds when you flip the Parity Switch like this:

"Taking action and buying this is better than doing nothing."

Your "competition" often takes the form of objections to the sale — which you can anticipate, prepare for and answer in your copy!

Whatever you do and whatever you say, DO NOT leave a single lingering question or doubt in your customers' minds about you as the best possible solution for their problem (or most rewarding route to achieving their goal).

To Turn On The Parity Switch, Answer These Questions In Your Sales Copy:

(i) Does my sales copy offer the useful features, desirable benefits and lasting results that my potential customers are used to seeing from my competition?

(ii) Do I have 2-3 aspects of my offer that instantly raises my status above my competition? What benefits can I show that my competition has not provided?

(iii) What excuses about their lack of ability, self-discipline, creativity etc. can keep potential customers from becoming actual customers? How can I assure them (through an FAQ, for instance) that my product or service "works around" those excuses?

The Parity Switch At Work: An Example

This live training not only gives you easily implementable insights such as [A, B and C] but it also gives you counter-intuitive strategies like [X, Y and Z] — you won't find these anywhere else online or off!

How this offer covers all aspects that the potential customer is used to seeing in the competition:

This training not only gives you easily implementable insights such as [A, B and C]…

How this offer elevates the product's status above the competition:

…but it also gives you counter-intuitive strategies like [X, Y and Z] — you won't find these anywhere else online or off!

Swipe This Switch:

- Use phrases like "Let's do the math" and "You be the judge" to demonstrate how you *want* them to make the most beneficial decision.
- Make sure your pitch covers all aspects of the product or service that customers will see in a competitor's pitch.
- Go above and beyond by drawing comparisons between the differentiating features of your product or service and how the competition falls short in relieving your customers' pain points.

PERSUASION SWITCH #4
THE CURIOSITY SWTICH

Humans:

We're nosy little fucks.

Since the dawn of womankind (okay, and *man*kind), curiosity has proven itself to be an exceptionally powerful and innately human emotion.

Without curiosity, there would be no psychology-backed, neuroscience-proven persuasion — or *any* science at all for that matter!

Curiosity is impossible to ignore and impossible to resist.

When the unknown is unknown, we CRAVE to make it known.

To figure it out.

To see what's going on.

To find out how we might be missing out.

If you manage to take a jab at your customers' sense of curiosity, you might as well check your inbox, because the payment notifications are going to fill it up FAST.

But there is a danger here…

When you get your customers curious, you have their attention.

When you have their attention, you absolutely MUST deliver.

The problem that most sales and persuasion "experts" cannot seem to shake off their advice is the one-off recommendation to use fantastic curiosity-evoking headlines…and stopping there.

Sure, you got folks to open the email.

Sure, you got them to click.

Sure, you got them to hit "play" on your video.

Then what?

You need to sustain people's attention. Hold their focus on your message and get them to devour it without stopping.

With the Curiosity Switch, you're all set to do both.

To Turn On The Curiosity Switch, Make Sure Your Copy Answers These Questions:

(i) Does my headline or title make my potential customer think, "I HAVE to know what happens next"?

(ii) Am I using enticing phrases in my supporting copy to hold their attention and motivate them to keep reading or watching?

The Curiosity Switch At Work: An Example

"What my obese mom taught me about eating healthy."

Now, you must be wondering how that's possible…

How this headline creates curiosity:

What my obese mom taught me about eating healthy…

How an enticing phrase keeps them reading past the headline:

Now, you must be wondering how that's possible…

Swipe This Switch:

- Use gotta-know-the-answer phrases like, "The biggest mistake you don't know you're making", "What they don't tell you" and "I have a secret sauce that works" to fire up the Curiosity Switch in headings and subject lines (but don't clickbait people with a headline that has nothing to do with the content!).

- Create a logic gap in your descriptions or subject lines with oddly contradictory phrases like, "What my convict father taught me about ethics".

- Use understanding-connector phrases like, "I know what you're thinking", "I'm sure you'll agree" and "What would this be worth to you?" in your copy to sustain attention and cultivate a bond between them and you.

- In emails, keep your audience emotionally invested in your message by asking them to shoot over a response to a statement or question you posed.

PERSUASION SWITCH #5
THE URGENCY SWITCH

If the Persuasion Switches were guys, the Urgency Switch would be the cool, impossibly attractive, long-haired biker type with that "love 'em and leave 'em" attitude.

Yes, the Bad Boy of the Persuasion Switches — it's got a bad rep.

That's why we have to be very, very, VERY careful when switching on the Urgency.

Because this Switch works due to the fact that we humans all suffer from the fear of being left out.

Being left behind.

Being out of the loop.

Being looked over.

Being forgotten.

That's why it's so powerful — and so dangerous. You can probably tell where I'm going with this...

This Switch takes advantage of the fact that there isn't enough to go around (the scarcity mindset) so you'd better grab whatever is on sale NOW!

This Switch activates the fear that they won't end up winning "The Miss Congeniality" award.

Whenever you see copy like the samples below, someone is trying to flip the Urgency Switch on your lovely ass:

"Get this before time runs out."

"Limited spots available. Book your session now!"

"This offer will go away in 24 hours. Join now!"

Notice the scarcity and fear at play in these sentences (or as they are known in the copywriting world, "Calls To Action" or CTA's).

This tactic can get old. FAST.

Across most industries and in just about every country on the planet, customers are becoming more and more sophisticated, which means scarcity-based tactics can only take you so far.

If you sell an "evergreen" product or self-study eCourse as a passive income generator, you can't use this type of urgency to get your customers to buy.

Why? Because products like essential oils or earrings or evergreen eCourses don't just "run out".

If there is no real time limit – or any other sort of legitimate limit – you cannot trick your customers into thinking there is. Not in the Information Age where bold claims can be instantly debunked with 30 seconds of Googling (or hitting the Refresh button to see the timer restart!).

If you try to create a sense of scarcity when there's none through slick sales page trickery, they'll know you're faking it.

And fakers are always punished with an empty bank account (and possibly bans from their hosting service as well – double whammy).

Luckily, *Mass Persuasion Method* takes this into account.

As you guessed, there IS an ethical way to flip the Urgency Switch without falsifying scarcity to motivate purchases out of fear.

Your job to make that happen? Hone in on the other all-too-human need called "instant gratification".

When promoting your products or services, work in urgency AND scarcity by offering enticing extras that they can't do without.

Tap into FOMO (Fear of Missing Out)! This creates *real* urgency that pushes potential buyers off the fence to whip out their credit cards for you NOW.

To Flip The Urgency Switch, Make Sure Your Copy Answers These Questions:

(i) Am I attracting people with the promise of instant gratification if they buy now (rather than put it off until later, AKA never)?

(ii) Am I introducing FOMO by offering an irresistible benefit or promising a tangible result that is *only* available to people who act now?

The Urgency Switch At Work: An Example

Don't miss this chance to become a Master Persuader in less time than it took for you to learn how to ride a bike. Anyone who buys this program in the next 24 hours will receive a special Copy Makeover where I'll personally polish your copy to make it absolutely irresistible for your ideal client.

How Instant Gratification makes this offer's promise irresistible:

Don't miss this chance to become a Master Persuader in less time than it took for you to learn how to ride a bike...

How a time deadline leverages FOMO to create real urgency *and* scarcity:

...Anyone who buys this program in the next 24 hours will receive a special Copy Makeover where I'll personally polish your copy to make it absolutely irresistible to your ideal client.

Swipe This Switch:

- Limit the number of spots available for your online program or service to create exclusivity around your brand.
- Close your virtual shopping cart when you say you will.

- Cultivate a legitimate fear of losing out on an incredible opportunity by including a "last chance" message in your emails (i.e. "This is your last chance to get this course at $49. Price goes up to $149 tomorrow.").

- Plug Instant Gratification into your offer so your audience worries that they'll regret missing out on a life-changing solution if they don't get off the fence and buy.

PERSUASION SWITCH #6
THE DESIRABILITY SWITCH

The grass *can* be greener on your side.

More specifically, on your *customers'* side.

Because you and your product or service will make that happen.

That's where the Desirability Switch comes into the picture to benefit both you *and* your customers.

This Switch allows your customers to visualize a beautiful, new tomorrow...

A tomorrow where they will be gorgeous, fit, rich, happy or whatever it is they're trying to achieve that you can help them do (or become).

With the Desirability Switch, you are painting a "word picture" of what their life is going to look and feel like after they've used your product or worked with you.

The best part about this Switch is its immediate effect on your buyers' psyche — "I HAVE to have this NOW!"

The Desirability Switch uses "magnetism" to persuade because your customers feel themselves drawn toward a better future.

In that way, it's the exact opposite of the Urgency Switch, where you give customers an urge (pun, see?) to escape that feeling of missing out on something.

The Desirability Switch utilizes emotion-rich, future-oriented copy to pull customers toward what they really, truly want.

They can see it.

They can feel it.

The can almost taste it.

And so they want it.

At that point, your asking price is all but irrelevant.

To Flip The Desirability Switch, Make Sure Your Copy Answers These Questions:

(i) Am I painting a "life after" picture that allows customers to see how life changes for the better after buying my product or service?

(ii) Am I vividly describing the ideal state of being that my customers can unlock…if only they buy?

The Desirability Switch At Work: An Example

Imagine how your life will change when you get a good night's sleep night after night and feel 10 years younger because you have truckloads of energy (to spare) all day, every day. What would it feel like to leap out of bed and be ready to go instead of hitting the snooze button for the tenth time?

How the copy paints a word portrait of "life after":

Imagine how your life will change when you get a good night's sleep night after night and feel 10 years younger because you have truckloads of energy (to spare) all day, every day...

How vivid descriptions allows the buyer to visualize their ideal state:

...What would it feel like to leap out of bed and be ready to go instead of hitting the snooze button for the tenth time?

Swipe This Switch:

- Describe what a regular day might look like for them after they've used your solution and are reaping the rewards.

- Use sentence openers like, "Imagine this day with me..." and "How would you feel if..."

- Work in a "No Questions Asked Guarantee" into your offer so you relieve customers' concern they'll be out of their money (and out of luck) if your solution doesn't work.

PERSUASION SWITCH #7
THE EDUTAINMENT SWITCH

If you're anything like me, you probably remember falling asleep with your eyes open in school when one of those book-smart but boring-in-real-life teachers droned on and on about History or Science.

Remember that feeling. Hold on to it with me for a second.

Because feeling brain-drainingly bored doesn't end with long-winded teachers and short attention-spanned students.

Most people live deathly boring lives — a sad statement that seems truer the more you think about it...

Most people wake up in the morning and stumble into a morning routine that keeps them from meditating on the thought that plays on repeat inside their brains:

"Another boring day. Just like yesterday. Just like tomorrow. Kill me now!"

Maybe an exaggeration — but you catch my drift.

If your customers are bored, they don't learn (I challenge you to remember a single relevant thing from one of those boring classes in school).

When your customers don't learn, they can't improve their lives using your ideas, methods or services.

When they can't improve their lives, they're not going to blame themselves.

Can I get an, "Uh-oh..."?

Just as I knew whose fault it was that I dozed off in class, your customers are going to place the blame squarely on you and your boring product or service.

They'll claim your stuff doesn't work, and you'll find yourself with a one-way ticket to Refund City courtesy of the troll fiend Buyer's Remorse.

Fortunately, I know a detour that keeps you from getting there.

It's called the Edutainment Switch.

When your customers are having fun, they can get out of their own way and actually LEARN something — in this case, learn what it will take to get the results they want...then actually follow through!

If you can lighten up someone's day with an email or a Facebook post or a video module that makes them smile or laugh, they're going to love you — and love learning from you.

After launching my very first online program in 2014 – 3Days3K – I got email after email from customers pinging my inbox, all telling me that my sales page literally made them LOL.

#Win #BigTime

More than one buyer even told me they re-read the sales page several times — they enjoyed it THAT much.

A freakin' sales page, people!

Most people run from sales pages like they're escaping a ski mask wearing murderer in a teen horror B-movie.

Even though practically no one in my field knew of my existence when I launched 3Days3K, sales went through the roof (so much so that I had to get a new one).

All because I flipped the fuck out of the Edutainment Switch!

The fact is, yes people want to learn, but they also want to be entertained.

That's why this Switch works especially well for products or services that have an inherent education focus (i.e., teaching a new skill, learning vast amounts of complex information etc.)

Despite what we want to believe, the average person doesn't consume our ideas, message or methods through the filter of pure logic alone.

Even a product that can make every single buyer gorgeous, fit, rich or happy won't fly if your presentation style is a "just the facts" approach.

As I said in Chapter 1, we don't live in a world where good ideas sell themselves.

Only when you tickle people's sense of humor can you capture the attention of the easily bored student that exists inside their heads long enough to teach that student something that will make them HAPPY to buy from you.

To Flip The Edutainment Switch, Make Sure Your Copy Answers These Questions:

(i) Am I poking fun at relatable regular life events and inserting self-deprecating jokes into my message at unexpected times?

(ii) Do I link back to my topics after describing an interesting life event, whipping out a joke or bringing people to a thigh-slapping punchline?

The Edutainment Switch At Work: An Example

My 2 year-old puked all over my keyboard (I know, I was horrified too!) and I haven't emailed you for a while. You might have forgotten who I am and that's exactly what I DON'T want happening to you. That's why today, I'm asking a billion dollar question — how often should you email your subscribers?

How a regular life event introduces the self-deprecating joke:

My 2 year-old puked all over my keyboard (I know, I was horrified too!) and I haven't emailed you for a while. You might have forgotten who I am...

How the personal story cleverly links back to the topic:

…And that's exactly what I DON'T want happening to you which is why today, I'm asking a billion dollar question — how often should you email your subscribers?

Swipe This Switch:

- Share relevant anecdotes from your life in your emails, blog posts, social media posts and your website copy that can easily transition to your topics.

- Package raw information in an entertaining way to make learning FUN (webinars are the ideal place to do this).

- Pump some self-deprecating humor into your messaging, even if you think you have a weird sense of humor. I promise you, there WILL be people who will totally dig your jokes.

- Think of some random, regular life events and link them to topics in your niche (this works well with social media posts especially).

- Use current events in the sports, music or entertainment industry and tie those to a topic in your business' messaging to produce content that is genuinely useful and culturally relevant.

PERSUASION SWITCH #8
THE RELATABILITY SWITCH

You are going to hate me for the cliché I'm about to use…

But I promise that you'll love me again (and feel like baking me a batch of Nutella-covered bon-bon's) when I explain *why* I used the cliché.

Ready?

"People buy from people they know, like and trust."

Ugh...

So basic you could puke.

Now let me ask you something:

How?

As in, *how* do you make people know, like and trust you…

And then *BUY* from you…

When they haven't met you in person yet?

When they don't know anything about your life besides what you put in front of them on the internet?

When they haven't seen inside your program or don't have a clue what it's like to work with you?

When they've already felt jaded by an "authentic" online "expert" who peddled drivel with less substance than a Top 10 Ways To Earn Money article?

I'll tell you how:

The Relatability Switch.

That's how.

Because the moment you flip this Switch, total strangers cannot help but feel like you're someone that they *already* know, like and trust.

Obviously the Know-Like-Trust factor makes up the 3 most important elements that drive a sale.

But that doesn't mean your life story has to be identical or even somewhat similar to your customers' to flip the Relatability Switch.

Because Relatability in the context of *Mass Persuasion Method* is not dependent on outside circumstances, it's based on the forging of a deep, heartfelt connection.

What do you and your audience have in common that motivates you every day?

What do you both HATE about the way unethical shmucks in your industry peddle their version of snake oil?

What aspects of your "present day" life are exactly like the "future" life your customers want more than anything else?

See what I mean? The Relatability Switch doesn't get flipped when you write, "Just like you, I blah blah blah..."

That one is way too obvious — and way too easy to lie about.

There has to be true meaning like the examples above.

See? Promised you would love me again! Now how about those bon-bon's...

To Flip The Relatability Switch, Make Sure Your Copy Answers These Questions:

(i) Am I using the art of story to get people emotionally invested in my life and why I care about theirs?

(ii) Am I creating relatability touch points throughout my copy and messaging so that my audience views me as a "real person" and not an airbrushed online personality who views them as objects to use and abuse to get rich?

The Relatability Switch At Work: An Example

Have you ever been in that situation...you know the one... you walk into a party or a networking event and every single soul there is a complete stranger? How did that make you feel? Frozen? Terrified? Suddenly feeling an irresistible urge to jump out the nearest window? I know that feeling because it happened to me just a week ago...

How a deeply personal story gets people emotionally invested:

Have you ever been that situation...you know the one... you walk into a party or a networking event and every single soul there is a complete stranger?

How Relatability touch points work their way in to create a bridge to the main topic:

...How did that make you feel? Frozen? Terrified? Suddenly feeling an irresistible urge to jump out the nearest window? I know that feeling because it happened to me just a week ago...

Swipe This Switch:

- Create Relatability touch points throughout your story and strategically expose your vulnerability. Show your readers you're a human and that you bleed, too.

- Dare to be real. Bare your soul. This puts your potential customers at ease so that when the time comes to sell to them, you'll have a leg up on the competition because you developed and fostered a true connection — one that goes beyond a transaction.

- Think of the up's and down's in your life that your readers can relate to. Share them without apology. Nobody believes the expert who appears to be 100% perfect.

Are you ready to flip some switches?

Because that's the whole shebang, the 8 Persuasion Switches! Flip them all, and you'll watch your customers fall in love with your products and services, your ideas and **you**.

But keep these Switches un-flipped, and you can expect to hear the sound of a thousand crickets when you launch, pitch or ask for the sale.

That isn't an excuse to over-populate every single sentence of sales copy with all 8 Switches, however.

My persuasion Best Practice involves adding all 8 Switches to my *offer* — through emails, social media posts, Facebook ads, live videos and my sales page.

A post in my Facebook group might flip the Urgency Switch while my optin page has 4 or 5 other Switches on it.

So play around. Have fun with the Switches. Get creative when you work them into your offer.

Because you'll be using them to persuade the masses.

I promise you'll be amazed at the results.

THE PROOF IS IN THE PERSUASION:

Trisha Condo
6 mins

Thanks to your wording, I have 90 webconversions to my psychic reading page. Bushra Azhar

Like · Comment

Bushra Azhar Woww Trisha Condo Thank you so so much darling for coming here and telling me that...you made my day all bright & glittery 💜
Just now · Like

Write a comment...

Nutella-Covered Nuggets O' Wisdom

- The 8 Persuasion Switches is THE fundamental framework for your business communications and online copy to motivate your customers to buy from you, buy now and buy again (and from nobody else).

- The 8 Persuasion Switches include the Prestige Switch, Believability Switch, Parity Switch, Curiosity Switch, Urgency Switch, Desirability Switch, Edutainment Switch and the Relatability Switch.

- The 8 Switches subtly but powerfully connect you and your products or services to your customers' day to day lives and their fundamentally human needs and desires so that they fall head-over-stilettos in love with you and your offer.

- Putting the 8 Persuasion Switches to work ensures that your customers will be happy to buy from you and *stay* happy — so you'll avoid having to deal with Buyer's Remorse (and the refunds that follow).

SEGMENT 2

MASS PERSUASION METHOD IN ACTION

CHAPTER 3

PERSUADE THE MASSES OVER VIDEO

Let's do a quick experiment.

Imagine that there's a camera on you, right now. It's focused on your face as you read these words.

Visualize the gleaming lens and the red blinking "recording" light.

Are you feeling anxious?

Totally freaked out?

Maybe you're super excited — thrilled at the thought of your moment in the spotlight!

Move over Kim Kardashian…

The first time I took myself through this little experiment, I felt the urge to jump out a window!

I ~~don't like~~ HATE cameras. I absolutely cannot stand seeing myself on video.

You know that "freeze frame" moment when you pause a video of yourself, and you look like ghastly with your mouth yawning open, nostrils flaring and eyes glaring?

No, no, no, no!

When I started my business, I had no intention of using video.

I had no idea how to write a video script.

Was having a script even a good idea? What should even BE in a script?

To say that I was "kind of uncomfortable" in front of a camera would be like describing a root canal procedure without Novocain as "mild pain".

But once I started experimenting with video, I realized that video-based persuasion works SO much better to captive potential buyers than any text-based medium alone.

Now, I'm a huge fan video. My reward for getting over my fears?

None of them came true.

No reports of people throwing eggs at their computer screens when they see my face. No emails flooding my inbox telling me that I look so bad on camera, they've gone blind.

Instead, videos are an asset to my business and brand — potential buyers come to know like, and trust me through 5 minutes of video (or less).

Compare that to the popular content marketing strategy of blogging a few times a week for *months* before reaching the cusp of "know" or "like".

Video offers more opportunities to inject persuasion into your message in ways that other media can't.

You don't even need a professional recording studio to get the job done!

I would know… I pride myself on working out of a closet!

Yes, even you – the one who breaks out in a sweat whenever you think about that red recording light – can take full advantage of this most powerful medium of persuasion.

CREATE A REAL CONNECTION

First, let's get clear on why videos are the quickest and most powerful way to make an instant, memorable connection with your audience.

When you are passionate about what you do – and I know you are because you wouldn't be reading this book otherwise – your audience of potential customers can see and feel your passion reaching out through the screen.

That's why we cry, laugh, scream in fear etc. when we watch good movies.

Videos for your business capitalize on this.

The best way to convey emotion and create an emotional connection other than through face-to-face conversation is to watch that emotion play out on screen.

This is why Robert Downey Jr. is so ridiculously rich and famous — not because he does video marketing but because he mastered the art of *portraying* human emotions on camera.

Yes, words on a page like this one can convey emotion.

But not like a video can — a single, short well-scripted video.

When done right, video can make your audience of potential buyers feel like they are your "inner circle" even if you live thousands of miles away.

You and your message remain in their minds and hearts long after the video ends.

And that's what we want.

That's what creates a true tribe of raving fans.

And raving fans become buyers — more than once.

That's how you build a business that simply cannot fail.

Now that I've convinced you to give videos a shot (I have, right?!), you probably wonder where the best place is to start.

I've got you covered!

Taking advantage of video-based online persuasion that leads to wave upon wave of sales starts with knowing the 5 types of videos you should be recording and promoting.

TYPE OF VIDEO	WHY YOU NEED THIS VIDEO
The Super Sexy Sales Video	**Video featured on a sales page to motivate people to buy (ideal for low ticket items)**
The Tempting Teaser Video	**Short video to persuade people to click and go to your sales page**
The Perfect Promo Video	**Video to get people curious and interested in learning more about you, your product or service**

TYPE OF VIDEO	WHY YOU NEED THIS VIDEO
The Excellent Explainer Video	Video that explains a complex product or service (allot more time to include easily miss-able details)
The Incredible Intro Video	Video to announce your presence and share your story with a new industry

5 Types of Video That will Take You From Video Virgin to Virtuoso

THE SUPER SEXY SALES PAGE VIDEO

By using that title, I don't mean you should appear with long cascading hair and a noticeably low cut top.

No, my darling buttercup — a sexy sales video is a video that *sells, sells, sells!*

That's sexy in my book.

Add a Super Sexy Sales Page Video to the top of every sales page (especially effective for low-ticket items!).

I define low-ticket as a price point under 50 dollars.

For products at this level, your sales page only needs these 3 key elements:

- A sales video (5 minutes or less) featuring your fabulous self
- Your offer's headline and explainer text (benefits & features)
- A checkout button to buy

That's it.

No need for a long story with song and dance explaining why you felt inspired to create the thing while floating out on a lake up in the mountains.

No need to dive deep into your customers' deepest pain points and hush-hush desires either.

Include those 3 elements above, and your low-ticket items will virtually sell themselves — thanks to the personal persuasion of your Super Sexy Sales Video.

THE TEMPTING TEASER VIDEO

Record a Tempting Teaser Video when you want to highlight an idea, concept or story related to the product or service you are gearing up to sell.

Unlike your Super Sexy Sales Video, your Tempting Teaser Video should run 90 seconds to 2 minutes — no longer.

With the Tempting Teaser Video, your Call To Action motivates viewers to click an accompanying link and land on your full length sales page.

Spend that short time tempting viewers to click the sales page link, and you are good to go!

THE PERFECT PROMO VIDEO

The Perfect Promo Video is a nifty little persuasion tool that helps you evoke curiosity in whatever you're selling (and turn that curiosity into read-and-scroll interest).

To that end, this video does "tease," but in this case you aren't flat out pitching or selling anything on the video itself.

With the Perfect Promo Video, you're just trying to get more people to know about you, your product or service and why it's important.

There are 2 types of Promo Videos to use depending on your situation:

- **The Concept Promo Video**
- **The Teaser Promo Video**

The Concept Promo Video features a useful tip related to your product or service that whets viewers' appetites for more.

For instance, let's say you sell a line of custom jewelry.

In a Concept Promo Video, you could share a fantastic tip on cleaning jewelry so it sparkles like it did the first day your great-great-great grandfather gave it your great-great-great grandmother on Valentine's Day 1884.

After you've shared the practical, easily implementable tip (Concept), it's Call To Action time! Tell your viewers to check out your line of Valentine's Day jewelry that's on sale for the next 48 hours only.

But if you go with a **Teaser Promo Video**, skip the tip.

Instead, you straight up ask people to check out your Valentine's Day sale…

Or opt in to your free newsletter with more jewelry cleaning tips…

Or join your free Facebook group for custom jewelry aficionadas.

I personally use the Concept Promo and Teaser Promo Videos before and during my own product launches — both work especially well as Facebook posts or even ads.

Remember, you aren't selling your product or service with the Promo Video. You are selling the *idea* of your product or service so that potential customers follow your Call To Action to purchase your product, join your tribe etc.

THE EXCELLENT EXPLAINER VIDEO

Not all products and services can sell themselves in a 30 second Elevator Pitch.

If yours is unusually complicated and requires in depth explanation so that your potential customers "get it"...

Then guess what — the Excellent Explainer Video is your new best friend.

In the Excellent Explainer video, you describe how you created your product or service, what parts / steps / features are included and how those all work together to benefit the customer.

For instance, if you're selling a 100% transformation eCourse on how to write and self-publish a nonfiction book and there are 8 modules over 8 weeks, the Explainer Video is the best type of video to use.

With your video, you could spend a few moments on each module explaining how they build on each other to ensure no step is skipped on the way to getting that book done and out the door.

THE INCREDIBLE INTRO VIDEO

If you're launching a business in a new industry – or your target market does not understand what you do yet – the Incredible Intro Video should be at the top of your to-do list.

As hard as it is to wrap our heads around this, there once was a time when no one knew what Internet Marketing was. In fact, there are still people scratching their noggins over it.

If you consider yourself an Internet Marketing Ninja and your services package takes clients' online businesses from zero to internet hero, you can whip out your smartphone and shoot an Incredible Intro Video that informs your viewers about your background, experience and what's new in your industry — and why they should care.

Publish that video right on the homepage of your website (and as a Facebook post or ad) as soon as it's done.

This video alone works as a gateway to usher potential clients into your brand so they come away from that first experience knowing, liking and trusting you as a credible expert.

SECRETS OF A STELLAR VIDEO

Step one, create a video.

Step two, stick it somewhere online.

Step three, watch the cash flow!

If only it were that easy.

If all you do is make any old video and wait for the right people to find it and buy, you will be waiting for a long, long time...for absolutely nothing to happen.

Yes, your videos *are* there to attract your customers' attention and persuade them to click the play button.

But no video worth sharing on social media stops with that.

Stellar videos hold viewers' attention long enough to motivate them to follow through on your Call To Action (buy your product, click through to your website, complete your Contact form etc.).

Creating a video that has this profoundly profitable effect on people isn't complicated.

If you include 5 crucial elements in every video, you will be able to hit the Record button with the unshakeable confidence of a pro.

STELLAR SECRET #1 PRIMING

In our noisy digital world of cat videos and celebrity gossip, the battle for your potential customers' attention is won *before* anyone even clicks "Play".

You see, just because a video appears in your Facebook ad or on your website doesn't mean your potential customers are going to fall over themselves trying to click it and take notes while they watch.

You need to gently and persuasively encourage them to click Play — and the right words will help make sure they do.

Above, below or next to your embedded video, highlight the **benefits** of what you talk about in the video.

This doesn't mean you write a list of "In this video, I talk about…" bullets.

What value is there in what you talk about? What will your viewers learn or be able to do after watching your video that is worth dropping everything for?

If you highlight the benefits in this way *before* someone even watches the video, you give them a reason beyond their own curiosity (or boredom) to watch your video — and more than just a few seconds of it!

They are *anticipating* value before they have even started watching. That is the easiest way to win clicks on that Play button!

With our Promo Concept Video, this is as simple as mentioning by name the tip or tactic you share on the video.

For one of my online courses, I primed potential customers to click Play with this text that appeared alongside the video:

"Click the video below to find out how a rotten burrito made me discover the eight persuasion switches that all need to be switched on when you want to make a sale."

WHAT SWITCHES TO ACTIVATE

✓ *Curiosity*

✓ *Urgency*

Here is a swipe-ready list of priming phrases you can put to use right away to work in both **Curiosity** and **Urgency** to get more clicks, more views and more sales:

• "Watch this video to find out why I was crying like a baby three minutes in..."	• Curiosity Switch
• "Click to play the video and find out how failing my law exams gave me the idea to create my so-successful-I-can't-believe it Iron-on T-Shirt Tattoos."	• Curiosity Switch
• "Pay special attention at the two minute mark in this video and prepare to have your mind blown!"	• Urgency Switch

These phrases are intended to get people to do just ONE thing — click that darn Play icon on the video freeze frame!

If you don't prime potential customers with a reason to click on your Promo Concept Video, then you've just given them every reason to click the back button on their browser.

It's as simple and as devastating as that.

In case you haven't noticed, people on Planet Internet are getting smarter.

That means a standalone video without persuasive, click-priming copy looks like just another promotional or sales video that nobody has time for.

The people you spent so much time, energy and money trying to reach will finally see your video and think, "Nah! Her flaring nostrils and yawning mouth are hilarious...but I think I'll pass."

You don't want that.

The only thing standing between your Promo Concept Video and the dreaded back button are your priming phrases. Use them wisely. And use them a LOT.

Let the list I provided move your imagination to come up with your own priming phrases that match your personality, style and context of your Promo Concept Videos.

That way you'll never be in short supply of reasons for potential customers to watch your videos!

It is SO worth it to take a few extra minutes to create curiosity that makes buyers unable to stop themselves from clicking Play and hearing you out.

STELLAR SECRET #2 DISRUPTIVE START

And so, your potential customer clicks the Play button.

They're watching.

And you're waiting…for all the sales to hit your PayPal account, right? *RIGHT?!*

Well, no. Your job is far from done here.

Yes, I know that makes me the party pooper.

But getting the click is only the first Call To Action you're asking of your potential customer.

There is no point whatsoever in getting people to watch your video if they feel bored after 5 seconds and hit stop.

Don't forget what I said earlier…

Your potential customers are sophisticated folks. They already have their defenses up because of the minefield of spam and scams that is the internet today.

Even though you communicate the benefits of watching your video, their defenses are still up — they *know* your video is most likely going to promote something or pitch something.

So, how do you shake them out of defense mode and into a more receptive mood?

You launch into a HUGE disruption.

I'm talking one they cannot *possibly* ignore, one that shakes them out of their "Don't you dare sell me anything!" state of mind.

This huge disruption needs to be surprising, funny or interesting — but go above and beyond. Whatever you say or do, make it so unusual, so uncommon and so darn unexpected that viewers are caught off guard.

"Oh my…I didn't expect THAT from a sales video…Now I HAVE to keep watching!"

That is the resulting thought in your viewers' minds. This imbalance between expectation and reality allows you to insert the suggestion into viewers' minds that they have no choice but to watch the rest of the video.

Because now, this video is getting GOOD!

Yes, I know this sounds a bit like a mad scientist's experiment in a dingy dungeon lab, so let's dive into an example…

Let's say you're a Mixed Martial Arts trainer and you sell online self-defense courses.

A disruptive opening line for your video could be, "Hey there, I'm Kat Caroney and I'm here to tell you the amazing true story of how a 100 pound girl beat a 300 pound bodybuilder at boxing."

There you go. I bet you want to know the rest of that story, right? So does your potential customer!

It's an obviously unusual, wildly contradictory story that people just HAVE to know how it could have possible come to pass.

WHAT SWITCHES TO ACTIVATE

✓ *Curiosity*

✓ *Desirability*

✓ *Urgency*

Here is a swipe-ready list of disruptive phrases you can put to use right away to work in **Curiosity, Desirability,** and **Urgency** to get more views and more sales:

• "Can you work 80% less and earn twice as much?"	• Curiosity Switch
• "How would it feel to sit on Oprah's couch wearing a little black dress next year this time?"	• Desirability Switch
• "98% of school going children are exposed to a deadly toxin that no one is talking about."	• Urgency Switch

Shocking, right?

Once again, I do in fact take my own advice — remember my example of the burrito and the 8 Persuasion Switches from the Priming section?

To open that video, I held up a picture of a burrito in front of the camera and announced, "Meet this burrito. This rotten burrito changed my life."

Disruptive. Unexpected. Unusual.

It caught people's attention and got them to keep watching.

That's what we want. Stellar Secret #2 can make it happen for your videos, too.

STELLAR SECRET #3 MOMENT OF TRUTH

Ah, the ol' Moment of Truth — or MOT as I like to call it.

Your MOT is your origin story, the tale behind your Tantalizing Offer.

Start crafting your origin story by answering questions like:

- How did you come up with your offer, product or service?
- What inspired or motivated you to create your offer, product or service?
- Where were you when you first thought of the idea (some place normal or more out-of-the-ordinary)?

With the MOT, you're taking viewers behind the scenes.

You're showing them the "spark" — the exact moment your idea came to life and kick-started the process that ultimately resulted in the offer, product or service you're selling.

People love origin stories. That's why True Hollywood Stories was so popular on the *E!* Channel — everyone wanted to know how Johnny Depp became Johnny Depp!

The MOT element allows you to stir up emotions and create a real connection with your viewers in a way no other element can.

Without the MOT element in your story, it's almost impossible to stand out from the crowd — a crowd that uses the same tired clichés over and over because some coach told them to.

That's why I want you to think of the MOT element is the key that unlocks "emotional selling".

Because it doesn't matter what you're selling, when it comes down to it.

I don't care if it is sports gear, pet food, weight loss coaching, business consulting, copywriting, web design or jewelry — you have a Moment Of Truth, so talk about it!

Think back to the moment you decided to stop *thinking* about selling your product or service, and you actually *did* follow through creating your offer.

Let your memory and imagination work together, and you'll find your Moment of Truth.

WHAT SWITCHES TO ACTIVATE

✓ *Believability*

✓ *Relatability*

Here are a couple of MOT phrases for inspiration so you can work **Believability** and **Relatability** into your videos:

• "When my first client had tears of gratitude flowing down her face – that's when I knew I HAD to go big or go home with this."	• Believability Switch
• "Before the six figure launches, before the 50,000 email subscribers…I sat on unwashed pyjamas asking the universe, 'What should I do break out of my soul-sucking 9 to 5?' The universe gave me an answer."	• Relatability Switch

STELLAR SECRET #4 DESIRED ACTION

Closing out your Stellar Video with the Desired Action element is not the same thing as issuing a Call To Action.

With a CTA, you are just barking orders.

"Click here… Buy now… Start today… Join now…"

When you include a Desired Action, you are explaining what will happen *after* they click, buy, start or join.

In other words, the Desired Action gives people a damn good reason to follow your CTA!

WHAT SWITCHES TO ACTIVATE

✓ *Parity*

✓ *Desirability*

✓ *Urgency*

Here are two quick takes on making the Desired Action be acted upon by your viewers. Personalize these examples to take advantage of the **Parity**, **Desirability** and **Urgency** Switches:

• "Read more details below this video so that you fully understand why this is the best solution and see why hundreds of people are using this."	• Parity Switch
• "You are 30 minutes away from ending the struggle for good. Click the yellow button below to get started. You'll receive your course login within 5 minutes."	• Desirability Switch
• "Only 10 spots available to lose 50 pounds without dieting. Imagine the joy of shopping for new clothes in a size you once thought was impossible. Click the button next to this video, and you'll become 1 of the 10. Check your inbox for your confirmation and login.	• Urgency Switch

Let me offer a few more examples.

If you are working on a sales video for a copywriting masterclass, you can close it out by saying, "Click the blue button below and it will take you to an order form where you can safely and securely complete your purchase. You'll instantly receive your Copywriting Secrets Of The Pros Cheat-Sheets in your inbox."

If you are launching a pet food product line, you can include in a teaser or promotional video something like, "Read the details when you click on the link below. You'll discover why hundreds of people are saying that Kitty Cutie Pet Treats are the healthiest snacks their beloved cats have ever had and how these Feline Kings and Queens can't wait to get their paws on it!"

As I said, telling people what to do does not cut it — not for a Stellar Video.

But when you tell people what will happen after they click, buy, start, join etc., you are tapping into a quirk of the human brain.

If your potential buyer can see herself doing something in her mind's eye, it becomes infinitely easier to persuade her to do that thing.

That is exactly what the Desired Action element allows you to do. By giving your viewers a "preview" of their future – by telling them what will happen when they will commit – purchasing from you is not scary.

They know the world won't end!

Their credit card details won't get stolen!

And they won't see their names on some unsettlingly long list called "People Who Fell For Online Scams".

Your customers are safe with you — so tell them! Reserve a place in every video script you write for the Desired Action element, and you'll see potential customers happy to follow your Call To Action.

STELLAR SECRET #5 HUMBLE POWER INTRO

Notice the title of this Secret is "Humble *Power*" not "Humble "*Brag*".

I've never been a fan of the pseudo-humility in that phrase, which is why I am all about owning your value and making a BIG deal about what your audience cares about, AKA not going on and on shamelessly reciting al the compliments your parents have heaped upon you over the years.

Yes, you can be humble when showing off your credibility.

But at any cost, don't sacrifice your *relatability*.

Fortunately, the Humble Power Intro allows you to highlight how awesome you are and why your viewers can trust you *without* coming off like an ass.

Win-win!

WHAT SWITCHES TO ACTIVATE

✓ *Relatability*

This fill-in-the-blank script is personalization-ready for you! All it takes is a couple of minutes to make this script your own, and you're all set to switch on the **Relatability**:

• "I wasn't always this _____being featured in _____, being quoted • in _____ and being called _____. In fact, I was just a _____, struggling with _____, wondering _____ and feeling hopeless about _____. And then one day, my life turned around completely when I _____."	• Relatability Switch

One final note about Stellar Secret #5 — just because the Humble Power Intro has that clever little prefix of "Introduction" tacked onto it does not mean you should start off every video with your credibility-establishing Humble Power bio.

Instead, showcase your valuable experience and relatable journey only *after* you have disrupted, distracted, and made viewers curious enough to keep watching.

STELLAR SECRET #6 LIFE-AFTER

A transaction is not a one-time event.

Yes, when a buyer commits with their credit card, they aren't necessarily swiping ever after.

But even though that purchase takes place in a single moment in time, the *value* your buyers receive thanks to that purchase pays off time and time again.

A week after buying… Two months later… Ten *years* later, your buyers still benefit.

So in your videos, do not sell your product or service short by *not* mentioning how your buyer's life will change thanks to whipping out that credit card.

WHAT SWITCHES TO ACTIVATE

✓ *Desirability*

✓ *Parity*

✓ *Prestige*

Here is a starter list of phrases you can add to that will flip the **Desirability, Parity** and **Prestige** Switches to make buyers realize the long-term value of a one-time purchase:

• "Imagine waking up every day…"	• Desirability Switch
• "Imagine going to work…"	• Desirability Switch
• "Imagine taking a walk…"	• Desirability Switch
• "Imagine this day with me…"	• Desirability Switch
• "Imagine walking into the gym…"	• Desirability Switch
• "Imagine how your days will change…"	• Desirability Switch
• "Imagine the frustration of wasting another weekend Googling the shit out of the internet, only to come up empty-handed. That's why my program includes…"	• Parity Switch
• "Imagine the confidence you'll have, strutting your stuff and getting those 'Hot damn, girl!' looks from your friends…"	• Prestige Switch

What a wild ride this has been!

If you include all 6 elements in your videos – Priming, Disruption, Moment of Truth, Desire Action, Humble Power Intro and Life-After – you can feel good about yourself because you have just produced a Stellar Video!

Get ready to have your buyers magnetized to their screens.

You know what pairs well with being a video star?

Becoming a social media star — specifically on Facebook.

You with me? Let's go!

Nutella-Covered Nuggets O' Wisdom

- Video is the medium that allows you to convey emotion and connect with your audience in ways that text, images and audio cannot.

- The 5 key types of video you should create are the Super Sexy Sales Video, the Tempting Teaser Video, the Perfect Promo Video, the Excellent Explainer Video and the Incredible Intro Video.

- Your videos are irresistibly watch-able when you include 6 key elements: Priming, Disruptive Start, Moment of Truth, Desired Action, Humble Power Intro and Life-After.

CHAPTER 4

PERSUADE THE MASSES VIA SOCIAL MEDIA

If you've ever dreamed of becoming a star and having thousands or even millions of people know you as a household name, I'm happy to report that you were born into the right era.

You may not make it in Hollywood.

You might not even make it in Bollywood.

But you sure as heck CAN make it on social media.

In the Information Age, just about anyone can become a social media celebrity — what spectacular news for entrepreneurs who love the spotlight!

But not all entrepreneurs crave said spotlight, do they?

There are those of you who read those last few sentences and can't think of anything but the word "YUCK" followed by everything bad associated with celebrity status.

If that sums up your reaction, I've got some tough news for you, darling.

If you cringe at the thought of seeing your name plastered across all the major social media platforms, you have a choice facing you:

Stop cringing and start leveraging the effective medium of social media to grow your business.

Or not.

Perhaps this will convince you:

When I said **effective medium**, I mean to say that it's SO effective that some entrepreneurs are using only one channel like Facebook or Instagram to build 5, 6 and even 7 figure online empires.

All because social media is the world's easiest way to reach the masses for a miniscule cost — or even for free.

Getting your message in front of tens of thousands of people a month, a week or even a day was once a privilege of massive corporations. If your advertising and marketing budget could not pay off the debt of a small nation, you had no chance of reaching the average Joe and Joanna.

In the pre-Internet days of the 20th century, only exalted kings and queens of commerce possessed the power to reach the numbers of people that any of us can today via Facebook, Instagram, Twitter, Pinterest and other platforms.

The times they are a-changing!

Even if you have never sent a Tweet, never recorded a Facebook Live or never boosted a post for your business page, I hope you'll give social media a try.

Because I intend with this chapter to show you exactly how to get people reading and sharing everything you post on social media — and thrilled to see more from you.

I'll explain how you can create an instant frenzy of likes and comments and keep people buzzing about your ideas, your message and your product or service.

These instant frenzy lessons are based on published research that reveals what gets people to take notice of something on social media — and how to inspire users to share what they see with their own friends.

In other words, I'll be giving you a backdoor peek at the science of viral social marketing.

As a result of this chapter, you will be all set to start posting share-worthy, buzz-inducing and sales-creating content on social media...

Even if you have no clue what you should share...

Even if you're absolutely stumped about how to get noticed...

Even if you have no idea how to get people to like your posts, comment, click your links, start a conversation, respond to your questions or all the rest.

Even if you're a Facebook virgin, you will navigate the landmine-riddled landscape of social media with the ease of a pro who knows what she is doing, why she is doing it and how her efforts will lead to Return-On-Investment.

THE PROOF IS IN THE PERSUASION:

 Jen Bro
3 hrs · Edited

After implementing what I learned from the first 2 videos in the free bootcamp, my private FB group engagement has gone wild!

Members who I've been trying to woo to come out of the woodwork are doing so effortlessly now.

I knew then and there that if just 2 of Bushra Azhar's free videos created THAT (which I've been repeatedly banging my head against the wall trying to accomplish for 6 months!)....I had to get in on the MP Academy if I really want to take my biz to the next level (and avoid checking myself into a mental institution!).

Thank you Bushra Azhar for your generous spirited teachings! You've lit my sales-self on fire again (and maybe for the first time!).

 👍 Like   💬 Comment

A word of warning to the wise:

The 8 Persuasion Switches from Segment 1, Chapter 2 are making a comeback, so I recommend reading that section again to give yourself a little refresher.

If you haven't read it yet (naughty, naughty!) go back and take a look.

YOUR FABULOUS SOCIAL MEDIA PORTFOLIO

I'm going to make this social media thing easy for you.

Every status, video, ad or post you share on your social media channels must flip one of the 8 Persuasion Switches.

Your social marketing strategy is literally that simple.

So, before you work your way into the dirty details of scheduling your posts and writing the accompanying copy, let's start with an overview of what each Persuasion Switch looks like as a social media post.

For your reference, the 8 Persuasion Switches are:

- The Prestige Switch
- The Believability Switch
- The Parity Switch
- The Curiosity Switch
- The Urgency Switch
- The Desirability Switch
- The Edutainment Switch
- The Relatability Switch

The Prestige Switch on Social Media

This post establishes you as the expert who can upgrade your audience's personal status in society with Prestige Boosters like more money, a hot bod, higher social status, a more beautiful appearance etc.

6 Examples I Want You To Borrow:

1) **Share "Feeling" Photos:** Share pictures that have nothing to do with your products or business but convey the prestige booster you promise. For instance, how Starbucks shares phots that convey warmth, and good friends (not just coffee).

2) **Link to a controversial blog post:** There's nothing better for eliciting engagement than a little controversy.

3) **Share quotes that speak to their hunger for elevated prestige point:** If they want to be thin, share quotes that talk about how great it is to be thin. If they want to look classy, share quotes that talk about classic fashion.

4) **The BIG Yay:** Ask them what is the biggest desire they have

5) **The BIG BOO:** Ask them what is one thing they would do anything to avoid

6) **The Magic Stick:** Ask them what they would like to do if they had a magic wand

The Believability Switch on Social Media

This post establishes your authority and allows your audience to recognize you as that authority — and also as the one who will help them achieve the results they want.

7 Examples I Want You To Borrow:

1) **Data is the king:** Share new, relevant industry statistics or date from your own tests if you run any

2) **Break some news:** Assign google alerts for your industry key words and share the latest news

3) **Product photos:** Work best on sites like Pinterest or Instagram. Think about how you can add a unique angle to the shots (e.g. an employee actually using the product, a customer-submitted photo, etc.)

4) **Share case studies of real people:** Don't just share a simple case study, tell the person's life story a bit and about her struggles so people can relate.

5) **Boast a Little:** Share good words people have said about you in a post or email (screenshots with names blotted out)

6) **Call the Press:** If you have had any press or media coverage, share these every 2-3 months (for added punch use Sniply to include a call to action leading to your site)

7) **Share a work/life balance tip:** Your people want to know you're a real person with the same struggles as them. Share your favorite sanity saving tip

The Parity Switch on Social Media

This post makes it clear that you are the industry leader who is tune with your audience's needs as the go-to person (compared to the competition).

6 Examples I Want You To Borrow:

1) **The crystal ball post:** Make a prediction on what's in store for your niche or industry.

2) **Beat your competitors at their own game:** Find out the best content in your industry (using tools like Buzzsumo and Social Crawlytics) and either poke holes in it or improve it with a commentary

3) **Post a contrarian viewpoint:** If you have an opinion on a popular or trending topic that's against the grain, post it and make an argument e.g. Here's why I think you don't need social media to grow your business

4) **Share any recalls or ugly reviews about a certain product:** This is meant to show that you have your ear to the ground when it comes to your industry and people will begin to see you as an industry leader

5) **Own a popular topic and add your two cents:** Take a popular trending topic in your industry and share your point of view on the subject

6) **Syndicate industry news:** Do a weekly roundup of most popular posts or stories in your industry and combine them in a tool like Flipboard

The Curiosity Switch on Social Media

This post "prods" your audience so they cannot help but read your post and not miss a single word — all because they HAVE to know what's going to happen next.

5 Examples I Want You To Borrow:

1) **Post a 'fact or fiction' question:** Let your people guess whether it's the truth or a myth.

2) **Blog post (disruption):** Ask a disruptive question related to your latest blog post but don't reveal the punch line. Link to the post

3) **Blog post (teaser):** Rather than just posting a link and summary of the post, cut and paste a particularly intriguing excerpt from the post to pique your readers' interest.

4) **The half-hidden image:** Post an interesting image (e.g. a before/after) or infographic and hide a part of the image using an overlay. Ask people to click through to see the full picture and link to a relevant post

5) **Help Them Define Themselves:** Create a quiz (or use an existing one) that defines their type. For example' find out what type of dieter you are or Take the quiz to find out how well you know vintage fashion.

The Urgency Switch on Social Media

Your post stirs up the feeling in your audience's guts that they must take action NOW — or they will miss out on something big.

3 Examples I Want You To Borrow:

1) **You are missing out:** Share 2-3 aha moments or love notes from buyers with the caption "This is how life is with <insert name of offering>"

2) **The next 10 minutes:** Give them a list of things that they can do in 10 minutes and then add "buying your product" or "checking out your blog post" as an option with the associated benefit

3) **What can you do with __ dollars?:** Give a list of things they can but for the dollar amount of your offer and then include one "buy---- " as an option with the associated benefit

The Desirability Switch on Social Media

This post inspires your audience to dream of a better future or a better version of themselves — all by following your ideas, process or methodology.

6 Examples I Want You To Borrow:

1) **Link to a case study:** Case studies are great for delivering useful info in a way that's often more palatable and actionable than a standard blog post. These also work great to evoke a feeling of "I want this" in your people.

2) **Best picture contest:** Ask people to share the best photo using your product or service and get people to vote on the best one. Have a giveaway for the best photo.

3) **Post a screenshot of an interesting social media conversation about your product or service:** Make sure you have the permission to post it or remove the names of people in the conversation. Add your own thoughts to the conversation.

4) **Imagine this day:** Share a small write up of how life looks like when people use your product or service

5) **The ONE big thing**: Ask your buyers to share the ONE big thing that has changed after using your product or service

6) **A Chance to Show Themselves:** Do a buyer showcase and feature someone who has had great results with your offer. Allow them the chance to interact and answer questions.

The Edutainment Switch on Social Media

This post shares valuable information in a clever, catchy or chuckle-worthy way that keeps your audience reading (or watching) long enough to see the value in the info you share.

9 Examples I Want You To Borrow:

1) **A what if game:** Post unusual what if scenarios to start a conversation…e.g. what if internet disappeared tomorrow? Or what if someone randomly sends you 100K without telling you what it's about?

2) **Ways I fucked up today:** Share some of the ways you have messed up a task. This makes you more relatable and also entertains people who love watching train wrecks

3) **Things making me smile today:** Share some of the funny things you saw — anything from a joke to a meme to a funny anecdote

4) **5 Weird Things about me:** Share 5 things about you that are not commonly known and ask people to share theirs

5) **Things that make me lose my shit:** Share your pet peeves when it comes to your industry — anything from the way influencers act or the way big brands do certain things.

6) **Quotes lots of quotes:** Quotes that align with your values or that are funny or inspirational work great (use tools like Word Swag or Quozio to create image quotes)

7) **Recommend a tool:** Share a (preferably free) tool or resource.

8) **A book is worth a thousand quotes:** Share a list of your favorite books on your subject matter. You can also share passages from a book that is particularly compelling.

9) **"Caption this":** Post a photo and ask people to come up with creative or funny captions.

The Relatability Switch on Social Media

This post invites your audience to meet "the real you" and read (or hear) the story of how you became the fascinating, credible person you are today.

6 Examples I Want You To Borrow:

1) **Behind-the-scenes:** Take candid shots of yourself, your workspace, your coffee, your kids/pets and ask them to post theirs.

2) **Slice of life posts:** Share a typical morning or afternoon goes in your life. Share the tiny details; the roads you pass, the things you do. Make them see it.

3) **Ask for an ear:** Post a tricky scenario (real or hypothetical) and ask people what they would do in that situation. e.g. "What would you do if someone gave you a 1,000 dollars for wearing a tee with their logo on it?"

4) **Throwback whatever:** Share pictures of your old website, old pictures, logos, designs, your first products

5) **That one time:** Share the most embarrassing, gratifying or enlightening moment in your business' history and ask them to share theirs.

6) **The first time:** Share a story about your first anything…first date, first kiss, first customer, first business idea, first hater etc.

The good news is, you don't have to have all 8 Switches flipped on in a single social media post.

That wouldn't be humanly possible. All you Type A's itching to prove me wrong, please don't!

Trust me when I say that a social media post with all 8 Persuasion Switches turned on wouldn't make any sense at all. It would come across as the rantings of a crazy person!

Instead, I suggest you create a Fabulous Social Media Portfolio — a series of pre-created posts you can schedule on specific days. Each post flips only one or two Persuasion Switches.

This strategy allows the magic of social media to take over.

With every post, you will get more likes, more comments and more shares.

More people will wander back to your business page to give it a like — then go to your website, opt in to your mailing list, purchase your product or contact you asking about your services.

THE PROOF IS IN THE PERSUASION:

Gwen Teske
1 hr

Hi Rockstars! Quick question: I used Bushra's amazing MPM steps and 700 people signed up for my free 5 day challenge. Bushra rules!!!

Okay, so 60% open rate, and about 15% active participants in my fb group. Are these normal percentages? Tomorrow is the last day and I want to lovingly lure them into my signature program (€599), but now I'm frozen. How many can I expect to convert? Are there any prognoses on this? Should I throw in a lower priced program first? Hope you can shine your light on this!

👍 Like   💬 Comment

Because of your Fabulous Social Media Portfolio, people will gradually know, like and trust you — and you will reap the rewards.

Even in this insanely fast-moving world of social media, that old faithful Know-Like-Trust Factor applies. Like Nutella on a croissant, it never goes out of style.

When you have a portfolio created, you can turn them into a merry-go-round of posts that you use and reuse in different Facebook groups, your Facebook Business Page, Instagram or other platforms you prefer.

Here is what a sample posting schedule looks like:

DAY	TYPE OF POST + SWITCH
DAY 1	
Morning	Prestige Switch Post
Afternoon	Curiosity Switch Post
DAY 2	
Morning	Parity Switch Post
Afternoon	Relatability Switch Post
DAY 3	
Morning	Desirability Switch Post
Afternoon	Edutainment Switch Post
Day 4	
Morning	Believability Switch Post
Afternoon	Urgency Switch Post

Mix 'n match these posts – and create new ones – to publish a delightful concoction of Persuasion Switches that dials up your Know-Like-Trust Factor to flaming hot levels.

Over a very short period of time, your Fabulous Social Media Portfolio will create a fabulous positive vibe that fans and followers associate with you.

People who see your name or your business will think, "I really like what she says," and "Her posts are always worth the read," and "I know I can trust this person."

They won't even know why they love you — but they will.

Of course, YOU know why. You have been artfully and systematically flippin' Switches day in and day out, you clever bunny!

There's an extra special secret in the secret sauce that is your Fabulous Social Media Portfolio:

When you turn on the 8 Persuasion Switches with social media posts that offer truly valuable advice, tips and strategies, you will make your fans and followers feel smart.

When your fans and followers FEEL smart, they'll want to share your posts on their own because that allows them to LOOK smart in front of their friends and family.

They get to look like they're "in the know" as curators of useful content that is worth reading (or watching).

There is no faster way to make anything go viral than this.

Among the online ruckus of cat videos, overused memes and inappropriate jokes shared and re-shared a million times over, you are giving your loyal and growing tribe the privilege of sharing high quality ideas and advice with their own people.

Now, here's the great thing about *Mass Persuasion Method* when it comes to social media marketing — you DO NOT have to rely on chance!

You do not have to *hope* people see your Persuasion Switch-ed posts and engage with them.

Because there are clever, non-sleazy tricks you can whip out for every post in order to boost that engagement like clockwork (i.e. consistent and growing numbers of likes, shares, comments, clicks etc.).

So, ready to create a like-comment-share frenzy that gets you into people's minds and hearts to become your fan for life?

Because THAT is the automatic result of tapping into:

HIGH AROUSAL EMOTIONS

That got your attention, didn't it?

Sorry to disappoint — but these are not what you think!

"High Arousal Emotions" is a term that describes a physiological state of heightened emotional activity in your mind and body.

Okay, that still sounds a little dirty so hear me out:

High Arousal Emotions are emotions that keep you alert and interested. They make you want to know more and take action.

At the opposite end of this feelings spectrum, we have the Low Arousal Emotions. These are associated with passive behaviors — and passive actions.

AKA, reading your post and then doing nothing.

Content that caters to Low Arousal Emotions is not content that even *can* go viral, much less get noticed!

You know the kind of post I'm talking about… *A few sad cricket chirps interrupt deafening silence.*

The result of Low Arousal Emotions-based social media posts:

No shares, comments or likes — maybe one or two "pity" likes if you're lucky.

Now, don't get me wrong. I am not *completely* biased against cultivating Low Arousal Emotions.

Because a Low Arousal Emotion isn't confined to boredom or disinterest — Low Arousal Emotions do include pleasant emotions like serenity, calm and peace.

And that is the exact reason you should NEVER cultivate Low Arousal Emotions on social media.

The whole point of posting on social media is inspiring, motivating and moving people to *take action.*

When I say take action here, I don't mean leap up from their couch and do 10 push-ups or empty the overflowing trash can.

Taking action – in this context – is simply defined as liking, commenting and sharing your posts.

Yes, such an action only requires people to move their fingers to the mouse, keyboard or keypad…followed by doing a tiny bit of typing or clicking.

But I'm here to tell you how incredibly difficult it is to get people to do these things!

You need to shake people out of their Tuesday afternoon slump, Friday evening fuzziness, Monday morning blues or whatever state they're in on whichever day of the week.

You need to pull them out of their current thoughts and feelings with your posts. Adding a generous dash of High Arousal Emotions into the mix is your only hope.

Everything you post onto social media should be practically swimming in Positive High Arousal Emotions.

Positive High Arousal Emotions are exactly what they sound like — they make people feel uplifted and energized.

These emotions include:

- Surprise
- Delight
- Joy
- Enthusiasm

When you're posting on social media always stop to ask yourself, "Is this going to create feelings of excitement and energy in my reader? Is it going to get her pumped up?"

If your post doesn't do that, it goes straight to the bin!

If you ruthlessly apply this high standard to everything you post on social media – and only High Arousal Emotions make the final cut – you are all set to take over the (social media) world!

But don't lie back and open up Netflix just yet…

There is one more CRUCIAL channel that allows you to mesmerize the masses.

It's the dinosaur from the internet's early years.

We all know it.

We all have a love-hate relationship with it.

Email.

Nutella-Covered Nuggets O' Wisdom

- Social media allows you to reach thousands of potential customers at a very low cost — or even for free.
- Create your Fabulous Social Media Portfolio using the 8 Persuasion Switches from Chapter 2 to consistently captivate people with literally everything you post.
- Evoke High Arousal Emotions like joy, enthusiasm and surprise in your social media posts to create a steady stream of likes, comments and shares.

CHAPTER 5

PERSUADE THE MASSES THROUGH EMAIL

Oh, dearest email...

What joys and what sorrows you are responsible for...

What other medium makes people happy because they can easily connect to anyone anywhere in the world...

Yet also makes people feel absolute unadulterated loathing because they can easily connect to anyone anywhere in the world?

No matter where your opinion of email falls in this range of emotions, you need to keep something in mind if you want to run a highly successful, fabulously profitable business...

Unless you've been living in a cave up in the Himalayas, you have an email address — probably multiple emails, actually.

So does your brother, your neighbor, your great aunt Jane and Prison Inmate #3654 (yes there are email service providers that cater to prisons in specific locations... I checked!).

The reach you can achieve with email is virtually limitless.

Like social media, you have the world at your fingertips — a potential audience of buyers that spans the globe.

I've personally used email alone to turn an unusually large number of subscribers – who opted-in to my list via my website – into buyers.

20% of them to be exact — a darn good number if I do say so myself! Compare that to the industry average of 4% to 5%!

So, if you're ready to conquer the world with your ideas, your message and your offer, you need to conquer email first.

And I'm going to show you how.

THE PROOF IS IN THE PERSUASION:

Leigh Daniel ▶ 60 Second Persuasion
2 mins · Edmonton Heights, AL, United States ·

So guess what? I'm in this affiliate thing and my email (using Bushra's formula - 80% conversion! I'm killing it!!

👍 Like   💬 Comment

But before the how-to comes the how-not-to-do.

Consider this part of the chapter a friendly warning that will keep you from the terror of unsubscribe notifications crushing your inbox!

NO GOOD, VERY BAD EMAIL HABITS TO AVOID

My experience building a thriving 7 figure online business has shown me that there are just 2 types of traps entrepreneurs fall into when it comes to emails.

The first trap is to not sell anything at all.

These are the people who – for whatever reason – cannot bring themselves to mention their products or services in emails to their list of opted-in subscribers. Consequently, they don't sell anything. *(Duh)*

The second trap is to only sell, sell, sell.

These entrepreneurs think of every subject line as an ad headline and every email body as a sales pitch. No personal stories or endearing anecdotes — just cold pitches that deserve nothing but a cold shoulder.

Fall into these traps and your business has zero chances of growing. Either you will never even have customers…

Or you will make your customers wish they never bought.

Yes, email is about connecting with your people and keeping in touch with them…

But please remember the primary reason for sending out email to your subscribers:

To turn them into buyers.

Having a mailing list of passive readers is a dead end for any online business.

And please do NOT send your subscribers an email here and there just to "keep in touch" or "talk about life and where you're at."

This is a no good, very bad thing to do.

You should never be in someone's inbox unless you have something worthwhile to say.

If you sell handmade jewelry, avoid the temptation to send your subscriber list an email that's all about your dog and his trip to the vet.

Your email subscribers are on your list because they want to learn more about your jewelry. That's it. Your pet's adventures are rather low on their priority list.

On the other hand, sending subscribers straight into a sales funnel from day one with a series of automated emails – also called an autoresponder sequence – where you blab on and on about your products...

Well, there is no faster way to get your emails sent to Trash (and your email firmly placed on the block list)!

You might as well have said, "I want your money now!"

Fortunately, there is a better way.

Tell a tale instead.

EVERYONE LOVES A GREAT STORY

If you want people to actually open and read your emails, you need to craft a story that's actually worth opening and reading!

Your tale needs to be intriguing, interesting or inspiring — or all 3!

One caveat:

Make sure your stories tie in with the overall purpose of your email.

If you are writing an offer email in which you pitch a product or service, connect your story to that offer somehow.

If your email is announcing the upcoming launch of your e-Course, your story must make a connection to your e-Course.

This takes a bit of time and yes, it can be a drag. But it is SO worth it.

Because by the time your subscribers are reading about your offer, they feel connected to you as a real, trustworthy person thanks to the stories-worth-reading in your emails.

Let me infuse FUN into this email thing by doing the hard part for you — coming up with story ideas to prime your subscribers to become customers!

Use and adapt these 8 Awesome Story Ideas for your emails and blog posts to get people to open, read and click through your emails.

Customize these stories right, and people will actually look forward to your emails instead of right-clicking on the dreaded Delete button.

8 Awesome Story Ideas

Story Idea #1 What's On Your Nightstand

✓ *Activates the Believability Switch*

I don't mean your medication or your hand cream. I'm talking about a book you're reading.

What are you reading right now, and how does it connect to your business or to the lives of your customers?

How did it improve you — as a person? And how has that personal improvement carried over into the way you run your business?

This Story Idea works well to connect with newer subscribers and "draw them in" to appreciate you as a real person (not somebody showing up just to pitch a product).

Story Idea #2 The Strange and the Funny

Activates the Edutainment Switch

The good news with this Story Idea is that the story doesn't even have to be yours! #HardWork #Done

If a customer or client has ever shared a strange or funny story with you, make that story the basis of an email to your subscribers.

You don't have to reveal the customer's name or any other identifying details, of course.

Just know that passive subscribers become loyal, engaged readers when you tickle their funny bones!

Story Idea #3 Later, Hater

✓ *Activates the Urgency Switch*

If you happen to get hate mail (don't worry if you do — it's a signal that you have, in fact, become a success!), don't hesitate to share it with your subscriber list.

Take a screenshot, share it in your email and make fun of the petty person to whom you can say, "Good riddance!"

As the popularity of tabloids proves, we humans love other people's "dirty laundry".

If you want higher open rates, start airing that dirty laundry ASAP!

Story Idea #4 Clever Comparisons

✓ *Activates the Parity Switch*

Ready to take advantage of flippin' the Parity Switch in your emails?

This Story Idea has you covered!

If you're a health coach, for instance, your Clever Comparisons story could begin with, "Last week, my neighbor told me about this health coach she's been taking advice from for two years. You won't believe what she said about…"

Then you "move in for the kill" by describing how you are and different from (and obviously better) than the happily discredited competition!

Story Idea #5 Sex, Love and Money

✓ *Activates the Curiosity Switch*

Everyone loves a story that centers around any of these 3 scandalous 'n juicy topics.

Hollywood wouldn't exist without these 3 storylines!

You don't have to share inappropriately intimate details, of course. And again, the story doesn't need to be yours — that's what family and friends are for, right?

So, keep yourself a little database of stories, tales and misadventures related to sex, love or money (or all 3).

When the time comes, whip out one of those juicy stories and transform it into an email.

Just be sure not to use this Story Idea too often or you'll find yourself fast becoming the email equivalent of a tabloid publisher!

Story Idea #6 Struggle and Strife

✓ *Activates the Desirability Switch*

Everyone loves an underdog.

So become one.

With this Story Idea, share a personal struggle you've been having or crisis you faced. Make readers feel your pain and taste the sorrows.

But of course, get them cheering, too with the story of how you overcame the struggle and made your way through the crisis valiantly (or not so valiantly).

There is no faster way to forge an emotional connection between you and your subscribers than by expressing raw vulnerability like this.

It doesn't even matter what the struggle or crisis is or was! As long as your story eventually ties back to the topic of your email – the launch of your course, a special sale or whatever you want subscribers to know about – you are all set.

Maybe your story revolves around managing (or mismanaging) your time, failing to say no to the 6th doughnut in the box (and it's the 6th box) or struggling to finally write that love letter to Justin Bieber to tell him you're his biggest fan.

Let your battles in life become fuel for sales-generating emails, I say!

Story Idea #7 Messy Bessy

✓ *Activates the Relatability Switch*

Messy Bessy stories are some of the most powerful on this list because they endear you to readers.

"Hey, this is a real person... Wow I totally relate... OMG I have done that too!"

If you've messed up in life or made an embarrassing social gaffe that you don't mind admitting to, you have an A-class Messy Bessy story worth sharing.

It's absolutely amazing how many people love to see how others have messed up!

This isn't a bad thing though...

Because we all need to know we're not the only ones making a mess of things. When you confess your Messy Bessy's, your subscribers feel a comfort with you, a sort of camaraderie that they just aren't used to seeing from any other promotional emails from your competitors.

And that experience is inbox gold — so mess up away!

Story Idea #8 Pivotal Point

✓ *Activates the Prestige Switch*

That moment…

That moment when everything changed for you…

In your business…

In your life.

That moment when transformation took hold of you…

And you never looked back…

Write about that moment.

Maybe the Pivotal Point came when you read something.

Maybe someone gave you advice.

Maybe you were out in a grassy field meditating.

Or maybe you just had a rock-your-world type of *Aha!* moment while scrolling Facebook's news feed.

Write an email based on your Pivotal Point, and that email will grab your subscribers' attention and won't let go. Trust me (I use Pivotal Point stories at least *twice* per product launch).

THE PROOF IS IN THE PERSUASION:

Lacy Boggs
20 hrs

Bushra, I've made $500 since I sent out an email 4 hours ago.

This persuasion shit WORKS.

115 Likes 9 Comments

THE TRIPLE C METHOD

Ever heard that it's not a good idea to pack a lot of information into a single email to your subscribers?

Ever been told that people are generally overwhelmed and drown in an ever-expanding list of unopened emails — so why should YOU add to that with an email longer than one or two paragraphs?

Yes, your current (and future) subscribers are probably drowning in email. But that's not the whole story.

The whole point of using email to grow your business is to write emails that offer value to subscribers and stand out from all the other duller-than-watching-paint-dry emails they get.

Incredibly eye-popping email subject lines are the first (and best) way you can stand out amidst the clutter of spam to be found in the average human's inbox.

By the end of this chapter, I will make you the Lady Gaga of subject lines!

No long sleeves and dull colors here — go all-out diva! Be SO different from literally every other subject line in your subscribers' inboxes going back to 1999!

Because all your subject line has to do is win a click — by beating out all the other subject lines screaming for attention.

Bushra's Note: *Want another way to motivate people to open your emails? Include a teaser at the end of every email! Give a peek at the irresistible nuggets your subscribers can expect in your next email.*

To keep my promise of turning you into THE hot commodity of your subscribers' inboxes, I am sharing my secret formula to make every email you send pop out in even the most crowded of inboxes.

THE PROOF IS IN THE PERSUASION:

The joys of skyrocketing open rates can be yours with The Triple C Method.

The 3 C's to use in your subject lines and email text are:

- Curiosity
- Continuity
- Chemistry

Curiosity

Most aspiring entrepreneurs I meet think it's hard to evoke curiosity without lowering your standards to the level of those "10 Celebrities Who Aged Badly" clickbait ads.

In reality, curiosity is the easiest element to work into your email subject lines.

Here's why:

To stir up curiosity, all you need to do is use wonderfully weird word combinations or WTF-ish statements that make people go, "Really? I have to know more about this!"

Some of my favorite examples of curiosity-evoking subject lines include:

Can you really trust your mom?

What Lindsay Lohan can Teach Us About Success

If You Don't Know This About Your Husband, You're a Bad Wife…

Remember, the only purpose of an email subject line is to get subscribers to open the message. Curiosity is the fastest (and easiest) way to make that happen.

Continuity

The first of three ways to work continuity into your email copy is to include a teeny tiny teaser.

For instance, at the end of your email (or with the P.S.), write a teaser like, "By the way, look out for the email that's hitting your inbox in 2 days…You are going to love the surprise I have for you!"

This way, readers are primed to read the next chapter of your email saga before it's even out! What better way is there to guarantee future opens than this?

I don't know about better, but here's another equally useful way to add continuity to the mix:

Go the next step and include your next email subject line in your current email!

If you're a relationship coach, you can finish off your email with a preview sentence like, "Check your inbox tomorrow for my email titled '10 no-miss ways to get that hot guy you like to notice you.'"

A third way to create continuity in your emails is to go the numbers route — write a multi-email sequence where each email is numbered.

Include the numbers in your subject line like so, "Tactic 2 of 5: How to Get Your Husband to Take Out the Trash Without Being Told".

If they've seen emails 1 and 2, now they'll look forward to the rest of the emails in the series because of FOMO — the fear of missing out.

And if subscribers missed email number 1 and your tactic in email number 2 is relevant and useful, they may even scroll through their inbox to hunt down email 1.

THE PROOF IS IN THE PERSUASION:

 Lacy Boggs
8 hrs · Denver, CO, United States

A little win for me/you Bushra: I used your webinar email sequence for my webinar today and had more than 40% of the signups show up and STAY for the whole thing. For me, that's a LOT.

 👍 Like   💬 Comment

As you can see, creating continuity is as simple as it is effective.

Chemistry

No, this isn't Science class.

Our brand of chemistry is all about creating a real connection between you and your subscribers so that every email you send becomes an essential read to your audience.

Our first rule for creating chemistry is to use your own name in the "From" section of your emails. Never, ever use your company name or the name of your business (if different from your name).

And don't be afraid to add your personality and flair to your emails.

Using hearts, stars or emoticons in the email subject line might work for you if they match your overall style and message.

Maybe emoticons make you want to throw up, but for someone else, it's their thing. The tiny vivid expressions are who they are, and they reflect their personality well.

****

With the No Good, Very Bad Email Habits To Avoid on your radar – and the 8 Awesome Story Ideas and Triple C Method in your pocket – you're ready to take inboxes everywhere by storm and *WOW* your subscribers by creating fascination, ongoing interest and value.

Your rewards?

Opens, click through's and of course sales, sales, sales.

You'll be making bank, grinning like a fool and helping your customers better their lives or businesses with your expertise.

I can't think of a better combination!

Nutella-Covered Nuggets O' Wisdom

- Email is a powerful tool to grow your business and engage with your base of potential customers — a global audience right at your fingertips.

- Avoid the 2 traps most entrepreneurs fall in to when they write emails (not selling at all and selling all the time).

- Use emotion-driven stories in your emails to truly connect with your readers before you launch into a campaign to sell your product or pitch your service.

- Turn to the Triple C Method – Curiosity, Continuity and Chemistry – when crafting your email subject lines so you pop out in their inbox like Lady Gaga at your grandma's house on Thanksgiving.

SEGMENT 3

YOUR SUPER PERSUASIVE NO-DEFYING, CASH-PUMPING OFFER

CHAPTER 6

UNDERSTANDING THE "NO"

Pop quiz:

Why do people buy?

I'll give you a few seconds to think about it (no peeking at the answer).

I'll wait.

…

Okay, what was your answer?

Did you come up with something like, "People buy because they need to. They need the essentials like food, water and a roof over their heads to survive"?

Maybe you took a more holistic approach and thought, "Well, we buy things we need like toothpaste and clothes. But we also buy things we want like movies, smartphones, bumper stickers and Nutella to make life more enjoyable or convenient."

If your answer was like either of those above, I'm afraid you get zero points, my darling buttercup. Don't worry, just about every single one of my clients got this wrong the first time, too.

Please go ahead and reward your effort with a nice, big piece of chocolate cake or other unbelievably fattening yet incredibly rich dessert.

In the meantime, I'll fill you in on the right answer:

People buy because it feels good to buy.

Yes, it's that simple and that profound.

This isn't just my opinion (though it certainly is that). This fact is based on the hard science of chemical interactions happening right now inside our skulls.

People buy because they experience a dopamine rush (dopamine is the feel-good chemical in our brains) every time we make a purchase.

When I say "feel-good", I'm not talking about the mild thrill you get when you happen to find a dollar bill on the street.

No, ladies and gents... We're talking about a major kick that reshapes our priorities instantly — a "I-got-to-have-more-of-this-or-I'll-die" kind of kick.

The high when you buy is hard to deny (hey, I'm clever!).

The purchase-induced dopamine rush lights up our brains with delightful signals that in turn create delightful feelings.

And we humans have GOT to have more of them — or else.

This is also the reason why you're probably not going to stop at just one piece of chocolate cake as a reward for you effort on the pop quiz (a story for another day if there ever was one).

Back to my point:

We buy because it literally, physically makes us feel good, which in turn makes us want to buy more...which in turn makes us literally, physically feel good, which...

You get the idea.

This chemically induced buyer's high is so strong in some people that they become slaves to swiping their credit cards to buy, buy, buy (there's *another* story for another day).

So, what does all this talk of brains and buying have to do with your business?

Because in this chapter, I'm going to teach you exactly how to induce and incite this powerful dopamine rush in your potential customers' heads so they literally cannot get enough of what you have to offer.

Imagine what this power can do for your current line of products or services!

Just imagine being able to give every. single. customer that raw dopamine rush so they literally CRAVE whatever you put out on the interwebs that has a buy now button.

Our starting point to do this may seem a bit odd — I freely, shamelessly admit it:

The powerful dopamine-produced "YES" is the result of identifying and defeating the logical *and* emotional reasons that people say "NO."

These reasons people back away from the sale are what I collectively call **"NO" Drivers**.

These troublemakers keep your customers from reaching for their credit card in favor of the mouse to click the back button in their browser.

If you have enough people letting the "NO" Drivers push them away from your sales page or your contact page, you are effectively out of business.

For good.

Full stop.

For that reason alone, return to this chapter as many times as humanly possible to make sure that your copy – and every sales conversation you have – addresses the "NO" Drivers.

THE PROOF IS IN THE PERSUASION:

Li Lin
Yesterday at 5:47am

2nd sign up and the first person I have never talked to on the phone! what a feeling!

To drive out the Drivers, we need to ask ourselves a question (like we did at the beginning of this chapter, but reverse it this time):

What stops people from buying?

Depending on the product, it could be any number of things…

They're short on cash. They don't have the time to implement or use a product or service. They don't quite understand how it works — or if they're even capable of using it properly.

Take special note of that last one because:

Limiting beliefs people have about themselves can prove to be formidable obstacles on the road to hitting the "buy now" or "work with me" buttons.

These deep-rooted limiting beliefs manifest themselves whenever a potential customer thinks they're not good enough or worthy enough.

If they don't believe they deserve...

A better body.

A Mercedes-Benz.

A rich, handsome husband.

A brand new pair of beach slippers.

...then they won't buy.

It doesn't really matter what the product or service is, how highly it comes recommended or how badly the potential customer needs it.

The consequences are oh-so deadly for your business because these limiting beliefs extend to their use of your product or service.

In other words, they will be afraid that your product or service won't work for them...

That they'll end up trying it and then it will fail somehow...

That it will work for other people — but not for them...

Because they don't deserve it.

If this happens, your customers will feel like they were "taken in" and now look like fools.

The fear of looking like a fool is the most powerful sales-stopper — more effective at keeping that buy button unclicked than even a price point 10X higher than your competition's.

GETTING TO KNOW THE FOUR "NO" DRIVERS

Your customers' fear of looking like a fool for buying something that works for everyone else except them is only the beginning.

There are 4 major "NO" Drivers that get in the way of a no-cold-feet, money-in-the-bank purchase.

Keep in mind that we don't have any control over the negative influences that took root in your buyers' minds years ago.

You can't wiggle inside their brains and completely change how they view the world. If they don't think they deserve the rewards of your product or service, you can't force them to believe that they do.

Yes, that's a bummer. But I am a Persuasion Strategist (not a psychic), and that means we DO have leverage over the "NO" Drivers.

Because once you know they exist – and what they are – you can write your copy and go into sales conversations prepared to drive the "NO" Drivers into irrelevance.

The Four "No" Drivers

NO DRIVER #1 CULTURE

By culture, I am referring to the environment of beliefs, norms and values your potential customer knew growing up.

For instance, if they grew up in a household or community that believes sex is evil and dirty – and they believe that, too – you're in enormous trouble if you're a sex coach trying to sell them a coaching package.

Because of the limiting belief that sex is evil, a "Yes" is close to impossible.

Here is a less obvious (but still revenue-killing) cultural "NO" Driver:

If your potential customer's parents raised them to believe that having substantial wealth is wrong or unfair, then a side hustle expert whose core offer promises to 5X or 10X their income is going to "butt heads" (or in this case butt beliefs) with that potential customer, and the chances of a sale are slim-to-none.

NO DRIVER #2 BOREDOM

If a potential customer has had firsthand experience with another expert like you – or bought a product or service in your field already – they may decide it makes no sense to go through a similar experience.

This could be because they're just "done" with that type of product or service — or because they're bored with those previous experts, products or services.

Whatever the case, if your customer holds firm about not wanting to go through the same song and dance, it's unlikely that you can make a sale happen easily.

NO DRIVER #3 OVERACTIVE IMAGINATION

Worst case scenarios.

You name one, and I bet you I've already thought worried about it.

I'm one of those people whose mind goes directly to the most disastrous thing that could happen…and I stay there.

If your potential customer is anything like me, you're dealing with a chronic worry wart.

Keep in mind the rational AND irrational fears of a chronic worry wart when you write your sales copy (or have a sales conversation).

NO DRIVER #4 LIMITED THINKING

This "NO" Driver is an extension of the limiting beliefs concept you read about a few pages ago.

Some people's minds (and even lives) are riddled with limitations which can take many forms such as:

- Low self-esteem
- Physical limitations
- Social limitations
- Financial limitations

These limitations could be real — or they could exist only in your customer's mind.

For example, your potential client may think that she's broke and can't afford to hire you.

Meanwhile, you find out that her family owns a gold mine — and she has her own castle in Denmark!

But the facts aren't worth a piece of moss on that castle if she thinks of herself as poor. That limiting thought limits your chances of closing the deal.

Also, moss is cheap.

****

Wow... That is a LOT to overcome in your sales copy and sales conversations...

Limiting beliefs, cultural norms, low self-esteem, poor experiences with competitors, worry that everything will go wrong, the list goes on…

But now is a good time for the good news:

You DO NOT have to be a rock star genius and tackle all 4 "NO" Drivers every time you want to hear the sweet, sweet sound of payment notifications pinging your inbox.

Because not all "NO" Drivers are present in every potential transaction. The key to your selling success is to figure out which Drivers are going to be at work when your launch your product or pitch your services.

Reference the list of all 4 "NO" Drivers as you write (or tweak) your sales copy or prepare for the next sales conversation.

That will keep you standing in your customer's shoes so you'll know what Drivers you will most likely face.

Remain in a position of understanding your customer. This is the first of two cardinal rules to religiously follow in sales.

The second rule is up next — so, get ready to make reaching a "YES" easier and smoother than you ever thought possible.

Nutella-Covered Nuggets O' Wisdom

- People buy because it feels good to buy (thanks to the dopamine rush in the brain resulting from the act of buying).

- The 4 "NO" Drivers are Culture, Boredom, an Overactive Imagination and Limited Thinking.

- Identifying the 4 "NO" Drivers that are most likely at play in your customer's world allows you to counter them in your sales copy and conversations.

- The number one reason your customer doesn't follow through on a purchase is the fear of looking like a fool.

CHAPTER 7

WHAT AN OFFER IS NOT
(AND WHAT IT ACTUALLY IS)

Your offer — it's whatever you have to sell, right?

Like a 6 month fitness coaching package...

Or a self-study eCourse to help kick customers' bad productivity habits...

Or financial planning services that produce tremendous Return-On-Investment for clients...

Or beautiful paintings of mythical creatures that fantasy genre lovers adore...

Yes, there are all *technically* offers... But the product, package, deliverable or service itself does not make up the entirety of the offer.

Because a knock-their-socks-off-it's-so-good offer requires a clever combination of components based on the psychology of persuasion.

Whether it's a product or service, whatever you sell has to present a Great Offer made up of benefits and features, pricing, a buying experience, reasons to believe and bonuses.

Together, each of these components works in your favor to lead your potential customer to the sale. That's why you have to highlight each of them in your copy (or in your sales conversations).

Components Of A Great Offer

BRILLIANT BENEFITS AND FLASHY FEATURES

If you've spent even five minutes reading about online marketing, you know about benefits and features.

But in case you haven't received a proper definition of benefits and features – or you've gotten contradictory ones – here are my easy definitions for you:

Features are the "surface" aspects of the product or service itself.

For example, if you're selling a writing course online, a feature would be your 5 minute HD videos that come with fillable PDF's.

Benefits are the end results of actually using or implementing the product or service.

For that online writing course, a benefit of the videos would be how their short length *doesn't take up too much of people's time* while the PDF's serve as helpful reference sheets so students can *easily remember and later recall what they learned.*

I do want to issue a word of warning here though:

It's possible you are too close to your offer right now to be able to see clearly ALL of the benefits and features.

Not a week goes by where I don't see a sales page that confuses the two (benefits and features) or leaves out the benefits altogether.

A good way to navigate your way around your own offer is to use the word "for" strategically — as in, what is this feature *for*?

Selling 5 minute HD videos for their own sake without any tangible benefits is not an offer that can stand up to even the teeniest amount of buyer scrutiny.

But what those videos are *for* (the precious time-saving element) is where the benefits come in to play to lead buyers to a click of the buy button.

For now, take some time to reflect on your offer's sales copy or conversational pitch. Even ask a friend to help if necessary so you can be sure you capture all of the benefits and features that will make a potential customer say, "Yes!"

THE PROOF IS IN THE PERSUASION:

 Colleen Arneil
August 17 at 9:44pm

Reason #6,892 to fall utterly in love with Bushra...

Sales Page before Bushra: Converting at 9%
Sales Page after Bushra huffed, puffed and blew persuasion kisses all over it?: Converting at 22%

Ummm yeah. It's true love 😊
Study this page. Look at the elements, the structure, the wording. Learn from it!! http://insider.colleenarneil.com/web-genie

I created the actual layout and design of the page using Clickfunnels.

PERFECT PRICE

Price is listed second here because of its significance as part of your offer, not because your pricing or rates are the second thing you should bring up in your sales copy or sales conversation after benefits and features.

Not until you have highlighted every other aspect of your Great Offer should price be introduced to the potential customer.

But price is the second most important aspect because it **positions you and your offer in a particular category**.

Is yours a "luxury" product or service?

By that I mean, is your Great Offer only affordable for someone who owns a mansion by the beach?

Or does your offer's price make it accessible and appealing to the Everyday Joe and Joanna?

Or can just about anyone with 20 dollars in their pocket afford it?

Based on price alone, potential customers will know whether or not your product or service is even *intended* for people like them — so price your Great Offer accordingly.

SIMPLE, SEXY BUYING EXPERIENCE

The buying experience is more than just the customer clicking your buy button and typing in their credit card information.

A simple, sexy buying experience includes attentive customer service and – if you sell online – an intuitive website layout and checkout process that sends customers straight to their new purchase without any hiccups or confusion.

In other words, the buying experience includes everything…

…from the moment your customer clicks the "buy button" or verbally agrees to buy, all the way to when the customer receives the product or service.

There's just one relevant question to ask yourself when you're thinking about the buying experience you offer:

Is it easy?

No matter who you're dealing with – rich or not so well-to-do, famous and infamous, men or women, old or young, George Clooney or the aunty who cheers you on – all customers want **ease** in the buying experience.

So, tell them what's next. Tell them what to expect.

And tell them what every step in the process includes so they literally cannot mess up, break anything or get confused to the point they back out.

CANT-ARGUE-WITH-YOU REASONS TO BELIEVE

The entrepreneur whose potential customers actually *believe* what they tell them is the entrepreneur who sees those people become actual customers.

These reasons to believe are literally "the reasons your customers should believe what you're saying and buy from you."

These reasons can include your money back guarantee, testimonials and case studies (social proof) and your credentials, qualifications and experience.

These last three – credentials, qualifications, experience – build up your credibility in the eyes of the buyer.

Are you the expert that you say you are?

Are you truly experienced in the field?

Do your ideas, methods or products actually work?

And can you **prove** it?

Social proof from past happy customers goes a loooooooooooong way to strengthen your customers' belief in you and your Great Offer — all the better if you've had customers who are well known or respected!

If you owned a nail salon and did such a good job when Justin Bieber came in that he couldn't stop raving about his pedicure…

You had **better** highlight Justin's testimonial front and center in your website's sales copy!

Just don't discount the effectiveness of money back guarantees when you have testimonials like Justin's.

Because the money back guarantee has just one job to do — prove you have faith in your own product.

Think about it:

You are basically telling your customer, "Your money is safe with me because **you** are safe with my product or service — I believe in it that much. **I don't deserve to keep your money otherwise**."

Add as many reasons to believe to your arsenal as possible, and you'll find that customers believe your Great Offer really is as Great as you promise.

BLOW-THEIR-MINDS BONUSES

Finally we come to my favorite component of every Great Offer — **BONUSES**.

But I have to put my "What do you mean the Nutella jar is empty?!" sad face on for a second…

Because too many business owners and entrepreneurs I've met since launching *The Persuasion Revolution* consider bonuses to be some sort of afterthought.

BIG mistake.

If you, my darling buttercup, believe that bonuses are only there to add sparkle and glamor, please wipe that from your head with a clean towel and high concentration bleach.

Because it's going to cost you more sales – and therefore more money in the bank – than that belief could ever be worth to you.

I will go so far as to say that bonuses aren't just a component of the offer, they ARE the offer.

This is possible when you build your Great Offer on these delightful little guys I call "slam dunk" bonuses.

In an online course I launched (and sold out in 72 hours flat), I offered a slam dunk bonus called "The Story Selling Workshop" — people sent emails and posted comments all over my Facebook page begging me to sell them that workshop by itself!

As you can probably guess, I didn't sell the workshop separately because that would take away the overall value of my offer.

If your bonus is so good that people want to buy it separately, you know you've done your job and done it well. Slam and dunk!

There you have it.

An irresistible offer — a Great Offer to end all offers.

And now you have all the elements to create one yourself.

On to the next chapter now, where you'll discover how to match different *types* of offers with the right customers who are most likely to buy.

Nutella-Covered Nuggets O' Wisdom

- An offer isn't just the product or service you sell. A Great Offer is a clever and thorough combination of elements that smoothly and consistently persuades customers to buy.

- Your Great Offer's elements include worth-paying-for benefits and features, the rightly-positioned price point, an easy buying experience, reasons to believe you and of course the "slam dunk" bonuses.

- Highlight all of these elements in your sales copy or sales conversation to motivate your customers to make that coveted purchase.

CHAPTER 8

TASTY, TEMPTING, TANTALIZING OFFERS

I'm willing to bet that most sales gurus and other such illustrious beings would rather drink chocolate milk through their nose than tell you the truth contained in my next sentence.

The moment you try to sell anything to anyone, you are up against a crap-load of odds that work against you and reduce your chances of success to almost zero.

Bleak, yes.

But it's the truth.

So, why won't the gurus tell you this?

Because they want you to buy their program, course, e-book and coaching that promises to magically transform you into "Salesperson of the Year".

Now, I'm not saying those products don't work. The problem is, so many hopeful aspiring entrepreneurs buy this common advice without the right expectations.

They have no. freaking. CLUE what they are up against.

Here's a short list of the villains facing you:

- Direct competition
- Crappy copy
- Even crappier website
- Wrong price, wrong niche
- A horrible spouse who doesn't support you

Even though these odds can compound on each other to make a single sale impossible, I have a truth that will cheer you up and give new life to your dreams of selling out your products (or booking yourself all the clients you can handle).

Here's that hopeful truth:

None of these odds matter when you have a super-fantastic-deliciously inviting-incredibly awesome-knock-their-socks-off tantalizing offer.

You can and you WILL sell your offer… No. matter. what.

THE PROOF IS IN THE PERSUASION:

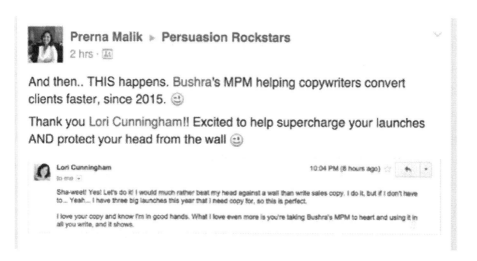

The smart, sexy thing to do is focus your efforts on crafting an irresistible offer that practically calls out your potential customers by name — like a tub of Nutella calls mine when I wake up hungry in the middle of the night.

Unfortunately, most business owners (even the ones who've been in the game for a while) slap together a pish-posh of text and images, call it an offer and shove it at their audience.

Then they sit around hoping for claps, cheers and the undeniably delightful sight of their bank balance skyrocket.

Instead they get nada. Zero. Zilch.

Maybe an email or two from folks telling them how crappy their offer is.

These business owners turn right around and blame the copywriter, the website or the way the wind blows.

But let me be a pal and tell you — even the world's greatest copywriter cannot sell your offer if it is inherently crappy.

THE PROOF IS IN THE PERSUASION:

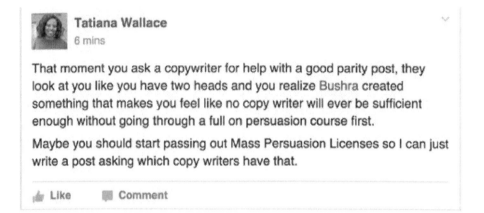

If your offer is not tantalizing enough to get people to actually buy, no amount of money you spend on websites, copywriters, membership sites, glamour shots or hiring George Clooney to sell it will work because the offer is just plain crappy.

But a strong offer – like the ones I will show you in just a few short paragraphs – can overcome all negative influences and all odds.

Your offer will sell despite anything and everything…

Despite the market conditions…

Despite the economic downturn…

Despite who is in charge of what country…

Your offer will sell.

That's why you need to create a super-fantastic-deliciously inviting-incredibly awesome-knock-their-socks-off tantalizing offer. Let me show you how.

TYPES OF TANTALIZING OFFERS

What makes an offer tantalizing is its *relevance* to the right people.

That's why you need to know the 3 main types of tantalizing offers and how to match these with your potential customers' current state of being.

Sound complicated? It's not, do not worry. All it takes is a little time (which you have already been investing through reading *Mass Persuasion Method*).

Before you know it, you'll be eyeballs-deep in creating your first, 10th or 15th offer!

The 3 Types of Tantalizing Offers

TANTALIZING OFFER #1
THE IMPROVEMENT OFFER

This is as "entry level" as it gets. Even though an Improvement Offer is tantalizing to the right type of customer, it's the weakest offer of the bunch — which means it's the cheapest.

Sadly, that also means it's the most common type of offer out there (where's the creativity, people?).

The Improvement Offer is an offer for a product or service that delivers a small improvement to the buyer's life or business.

147

When I say small, I mean super small — as in only 20% to 30% improvement, tops.

Improvement Offer Examples:

- Lose 10 pounds in just 2 weeks
- Get your sulky spouse to start communicating again
- Public Speaking Masterclass: Write, polish and deliver your 1st speech

These offers help — but only a little. They make your potential customers' current lives or business situations slightly yet noticeably better (and they're priced like it).

Improvement Offers are beginner, lukewarm attempts at creating change.

They're not as exciting as the other two types. There's nothing worth celebrating with flowers and fireworks here.

Let's take a look at the second example to see what I mean — get your sulky spouse to start communicating again.

If your potential customer is in a dreadfully dull and largely silent marriage where her husband says maybe 10 words to her every week, she feels frustrated, fed up and probably angry and afraid.

She's worried that her marriage is on the rocks. She's afraid he might be having an affair. She thinks she lost her sex appeal a long time ago.

So, presenting an Improvement Offer with a masterclass or ebook that shows her how to get her husband to start talking to her again has little appeal.

There *are* people out there who are a perfect fit for this Improvement Offer masterclass or ebook, but it would be all but a waste of time for this customer with bigger problems.

With a 20% to 30% solution, you are scratching the surface of what she needs, so there is no reason for her to drop everything and buy now.

The Improvement Offer isn't a lost cause though — I'll explain in a bit how it is the ideal option for building your list of customers (notice I didn't say subscribers), but the other two types of offers deserve a look first.

TANTALIZING OFFER #2
THE TRANSFORMATION OFFER

The Transformation Offer can be thought of as the Improvement Offer's "Big Brother".

Okay, maybe it's more like the Big Boss.

Why do I say that?

Because while the Improvement Offer promises that minor 20% to 30% change in your potential customer's life, the Transformation Offer promises 80% or more.

When you sell a Transformation Offer, you're playing in the big leagues.

Transformation Offer Examples:

- Go from frumpy to fashionable right now, with the clothes hanging in your closet
- Get a standing ovation at your next speaking event, even if you're scared to death of public speaking
- Learn to cook 5 authentic Italian meals in 5 days, like a pro chef

Here the promises are bigger, brighter and far more attractive.

The value is obvious. You're not just saying, "Go from frumpy to fashionable," you're saying "Go from frumpy to fashionable, *with the clothes hanging in your closet right now.*"

A fantastic offer because your potential customer doesn't have to run out and buy a bunch of new clothes to get that 80%+ transformation! No need to max out the credit card and fight the crowds for 5 minutes in the changing room!

With this offer, buyers get to *transform* or completely alter their look as other people watch them go from a walking fashion no-no to a cosmopolitan fashionista.

The same goes for the next two examples on that list:

You're not just saying you'll help your potential customer alleviate her nerves to speak in front of an audience...

Your Transformation Offer promises to get the customer a *standing ovation*, which means she will have learned how to deliver a blow-me-away speech with your training.

In this case, your customer may want to give a good speech, but she *really* wants – and is therefore willing to pay top dollar for – that standing ovation.

As for the third example, your customer is not just going to learn how to throw together a barely-edible, fast food-quality Italian pasta meal and call it a day.

Nope, you're promising that the food will be so darn good that dinner guests will think a pro chef prepared the zesty cuisine with world class ingredients.

150

Significant transformations, to say the least!

- *Frumpy to fashionable*
- *Nervous speaker to inspiring communicator*
- *Ordinary cook to pro chef quality*

Because Transformation Offers make bigger promises and require bigger price tags, it's your job to establish believability by peppering as many "reasons to believe" throughout your sales copy or your sales conversation as possible (see Chapter 4 for more information on "reasons to believe").

TANTALIZING OFFER #3
THE REPLACEMENT OFFER

If the Transformation Offer is the Big Boss, then our third offer is more like that guy in marketing who is always out of the office — but when he does show up, he comes bearing doughnuts and crème puffs.

In other words, the Replacement Offer is hard to create but easy to say "YES" to.

This tantalizing offer introduces an easy way out of whatever challenge your buyers are facing — and an easy route to achieve whatever their big dream or objective is.

The Replacement Offer allows your potential customer to sit back, chill and put your offer to good use – and benefit from is – without lifting a finger.

Replacement Offer Examples:

- Whip Out Your Email Sequences like a Pro Copywriter in Less Time Than It Takes to Cook a Chicken Curry
- 10 Out-of-the-Box, Good-to-Go Inspirational Facebook Posts You Can Publish in the Next 30 Minutes
- "WOW" Potential Customers with this Proven-to-Delight, One-Page Website-in-a-Flash Design

As you can see, these offers don't require your customers to do any of the heavy lifting.

You've done it all for them.

The very first Replacement Offer I launched, I named *The Email Persuasion Sequence (EPS)*. This product rewarded buyers with more than 30 done-for-you email scripts to use in their own email funnels, product launches and optin sequences.

I effectively *replaced* my customers' frustrations with email marketing with my 30+ scripts, which they could update or rework if they wanted — but each script was already good to go, as is!

I sold out the EPS licenses faster than syrup-topped hotcakes are gobbled up at a resort's breakfast buffet.

Now that you are casually familiar with your 3 new best friends – the Tantalizing Offers – it's about damn time to seal the deal.

But how do you know which one?

Or which *ones*, and in what order?

Should you opt for Improvement, Transformation or Replacement?

You take your Buyer's Temperature to find out.

That gives you all the validation you need to see your chances of hotcake-like sellouts soar through the roof and clear up into the atmosphere.

I'll show you how to get that outta-this-world validation – and take your Buyer's Temperature – in the next chapter.

Nutella-Covered Nuggets O' Wisdom

- You're up against a crap-load of odds when you try to sell anything, but none of the odds matter when you present a Tantalizing Offer.

- The 3 main types of Tantalizing Offers are the Improvement Offer, Transformation Offer and Replacement Offer

- Match each type of Tantalizing Offer to your customers' current state of being for maximum relevance (and profitability).

CHAPTER 9

TAKING YOUR BUYER'S TEMPERATURE

Depending on the kind of person you are, taking your buyer's temperature sounds either delightfully practical or deeply disturbing.

Time for me to clarify:

Taking your Buyer's Temperature does NOT involve a literal thermometer being inserted into various orifices (sorry to disappoint the kooky among us!).

To "take your Buyer's Temperature" is to understand exactly where your potential customers are at — in the Cold, Warm or Burning Hot categories.

The Buyer Temperatures

These 3 temperature categories relate to your potential customers' level of awareness of whatever problem or challenge they have (whether they're doing anything to solve it or not).

While this isn't an exact science, consider the Buyer Temperatures to be a useful metaphor to guarantee you launch the right product to the right buyers — every. single. time.

COLDER THAN AN ICE QUEEN'S HEART

Let's start with the lowest end of the temperature range — Cold.

Buyers in this temperature range have no freaking idea that they even HAVE a problem, much less the fact that they need a solution!

Let's say you're a wellness expert who sells guided meditation audios.

You know that scattered, unfocused, anxious and constantly stressed-out people can benefit the most from your meditation audios.

These people are the target market for that offer, but there's a problem…

If a potential customer's Buyer Temperature is cold, then she has no clue that she should be meditating.

Yes, she's running around all day like a little flustered chicken.

She's clucking and squawking and flapping and flopping about, uncertain how to get in control of things, feeling stressed and anxious as her mind runs a mile a minute.

One of your meditations will go a long way to help this supremely troubled bird, but here's the problem:

She has no idea she needs help! She thinks this is the way things are SUPPOSED to be.

To this cold customer, fighting anxiety, feeling stressed and losing focus all the time are *normal*. That's the only way she knows to check off every item on that to-do list!

So, there she goes again, no clue that there are tools and techniques (like your meditation audios) that can stop her squawking and flapping long enough to find inner peace and balance so she can tackle her tasks with a sense of calm and lasting, energized focus.

Potential customers with a "Cold" Buyer Temperature respond best to an Improvement Offer (see details of the Improvement Offer in Chapter 5).

The reason why derives from the Believability Switch.

Because you are NOT promising a huge, overpowering change, your Improvement Offer feels doable...

Realistic.

Useful.

Your Improvement Offer promises your customers a bit more comfort as they face off against the challenges of their current situation.

If you shove a Transformation Offer at an audience of Cold Buyer Temperatures, guess what will happen!

They'll get overwhelmed. They may not believe your product or service can help them as much as you claim.

They will react with, "Oh no! That's too much! I'm not *that* unhappy with my situation. I don't need big changes."

If I had a dollar for every time an aspiring entrepreneur has come to me for help, asking why their Transformation Offer isn't selling to potential customers that are as Cold as a polar ice cap…

Then actually doing the math on those dollars would lead to a depressingly large sum.

All an Improvement Offer should do – and therefore should *promise* – is a slight boost.

And stop there.

This offer is gentle, manageable and presents an attractively low price point for Cold buyers who don't yet realize how much help they will ultimately need (and want).

A NOT-SO-HAPPY MEDIUM

Simply put, potential customers in this second category are "Warm".

At this Buyer Temperature, your potential customers know they have a problem, and they know they should look for a solution. But for whatever reason, they're not super-motivated to do it…yet.

For example, if you're a personal trainer launching a 20 minute-a-day workout program, potential customers with a Warm Buyer Temperature will raise an eyebrow when they see your Facebook ad or stumble across your website.

They'll see your offer and think, "Yeah I've put on a few pounds… Yeah I feel kind of lethargic all the time… I should really do these workouts… Maybe I should bookmark this for later."

Even though there IS some interest in fixing their current situation, these Warm potential customers don't have that sense of urgency.

So, what's wrong with putting off a solution…right?

Hey, at least these folks know they HAVE a problem and need a solution — eventually. Cold Buyer Temperature types are happy to wander about aimlessly, frozen in old habits and beliefs (until you offer them a cup of cocoa, AKA your Improvement Offer).

Potential customers with a Warm Buyer Temperature respond well to a Transformation Offer. *(see details of the Transformation Offer in Chapter 5)*

Transformation Offers promise exactly what Warm Buyer types need to trigger the chase for a solution — a BIG change in a relatively *short* period of time.

If you cleverly show your Warm buyers how you will shift them into action – and make that change as easy as possible with unnoticeably small effort required from them – these customers will be happy to part with their money.

Notice the highly specific time-based promises built into the Transformation Offer for one of my programs in the online product launch niche:

"How To Use Buyer Psychology To Create, Launch & Sell Out Your Online Product in 35 Days Without Losing Your Sanity, Your Dignity Or Your Belief in Human Decency"

The first time I opened the cart, I sold 100 spots within 15 minutes simply because Warm buyers could not help but see my solution as a no-brainer.

Why? Because Transformation Offers take customers from 0% progress all the way to 100%.

People who were previously "on the fence" about tracking down a solution get a burst of motivation to finally follow through (and buy) when you present on a platter your Transformation Offer.

RED HOT MAMA'S AND PAPA'S

In my book (and this actually happens to be my book!), this Buyer Temperature is the most exciting.

Our third category of potential customers has a Burning Hot Buyer Temperature.

They are painfully aware of their problem and are actively looking for a solution.

They lay awake at night cold-sweating and thinking about their problem.

They spill coffee on their new outfit while ~~daydreaming~~ daynightmaring about their problem.

They park their car at the mall and can't find it later because they were lost in thought over (you guessed it) their problem.

They're Googling for help. They're talking to their family, friends and neighbors, trying to find a solution. Even the guy at Starbucks knows about their problem.

The type of problems I'm referring to are those that are **worth paying for, to solve — for good**.

For example, let's say you own an insect repellant company.

Your potential customer with a Burning Hot Buyer Temperature is the guy or gal who doesn't just have a "bug problem" in their house — it's a bug infestation.

Creepy-crawlies invaded their homes and took over their lives. Opening a cabinet reveals a roach colony. Termites are having a family reunion inside the walls, so the days of their home's "structural integrity" are coming to an end.

You can imagine how acutely aware of their problem these people are – in this case, it's literally right in their face!

If your business' marketing messages reach this potential customer with an offer like, "We will replace your kitchen cabinets and your infested walls with insect-proof materials so that no roach or termite ever lays its terrible dirty feet in your home ever again!" your customer's reaction won't just be to book your services, they'll jump up and hug you and kiss you before doing a happy dance in your honor.

The power of a Replacement Offer is its instant solution and the "Take my money now!" effect it has on Burning Hot Buyers. (see details of the Replacement Offer in Chapter 5)

Oddly enough, a Transformation Offer does not work as well with a Burning Hot Buyer because time is required to create the transformation they bought your product or service to achieve.

Imagine the effect an addition like "...in 35 Days!" would have on our bug-battling friend. That equates to 35 days more of suffering under the wrath of tiny home invaders!

That's also why *Email Persuasion Sequence* sold so well — time to implement and starting seeing results takes less than 35 *minutes* for most of the persuasion-powered email scripts, funnels and sequences.

Adding a Replacement Offer to your business model is one of the best decisions you can make to not only connect on a visceral, emotional level to the potential customers who need you most, but to create an army of success stories FAST — another advantage of the "instant change" aspect of the Replacement Offer!

Imagine launching each of the 3 Tantalizing Offers to your 3 Buyer Temperatures...

You TRIPLE your likelihood of converting a browser into a buyer when you have at least one Tantalizing Offer available for each of the Buyer Temperature types.

Launch an Improvement Offer with an entry level product, program or service package — perfect for people who happen to land on your website, don't know much about you or need a simple solution to get started.

Because they may have at least mild interest in what you're selling, your product or service has to offer only a small, noticeable improvement. Keep this Improvement Offer at a low price point.

Once these customers experience the small improvement you offered, you have effectively warmed them up. Now they're ready for an upsell to your Transformation Offer!

If they take you up on that and experience even a tiny portion of the promised transformation, their collective Buyer Temperature goes up SO high that a Replacement Offer upsell is your next go-to move.

With this tiered approach to selling and serving your buyers, everyone at all temperatures is happy — including you, who benefits from more sales than you EVER could have achieved by offering just one or two offers.

I call this "launch stacking" because every product or service you release can be directed at the same group of customers and potential customers.

In other words, if yours is an online business and you launch information products to a mailing list of subscribers, every person has the potential to buy from you two, three, four…fifteen times or more!

Instead of following the fatally flawed business clichés that goes, "Build it and they will come," where you launch a product or service and try to find buyers, you can start with an Improvement Offer.

Over time, you launch the next Tantalizing Offers that make sense — progressively warming up your subscribers so they are both painfully aware of their problems and insanely motivated to use your solutions.

Let me share a statistic with you: **20%**.

That is the percentage of subscribers on my mailing list who are also paying customers.

In the wild and wily world of online business, it's typical to see maybe 4% to 5% of your list become buyers — that's true even if you have 100,000+ subscribers and tens of millions in revenue.

Imagine what the Tantalizing Offers can do for a business at that level!

The same thing they can do for your business — multiply your profits, skyrocket your Average Customer Value and launch your products or services to people who are **ready** *to buy them.*

Once you have your Tantalizing Offers created, it's time to promote them.

Next up, how to do exactly that without wasting a single hard-earned cent or expending a drop of nervous sweat.

Nutella-Filled Nuggets O' Wisdom

- Taking your Buyer's Temperature allows you to present the right Tantalizing Offer that corresponds to the awareness they have of their problem (and how much they want a solution).
- The 3 Buyer Temperatures are Cold, Warm and Burning Hot.
- Aim to create all 3 types of Tantalizing Offers to match all 3 types of Buyer Temperatures so that you maximize your potential for impact on their lives and profit for your business.

SEGMENT 4

PERSUASION QUICKIES

CHAPTER 10

QUICKIE PERSUASION BOOSTERS

You're a smart cookie. So, I know you've already noticed this by now...

Persuasion has a life of its own.

Persuasion is both an art and a science.

Persuasion is profoundly human (remember the Switches in the brain?).

Yet persuasion can only be expressed through one thing and one thing alone — words!

Words are the life force of your online business. Without the right words, your offer is like:

- Spaghetti bolognaise without the bolognaise
- Frosted cupcakes without the frosting
- Oreos without the cream filling (an absolute tragedy!)

You get the picture.

When you write copy for your website, write a post for your Facebook page or write a landing page or sales page, the right words must be top-of-mind. Otherwise, you are wasting your time — and the time of everyone who will read your page and click the back button after a few seconds.

You can hire a copywriter to write everything for you of course – from video scripts to Facebook ads to email launch sequences – but that can get very, very expensive really, really quickly.

That's why I want to save your sanity (and your money) by equipping you with the essential tools for writing oh-so persuasively.

I get truckloads of questions via email (I mean literally, *truckloads*) on this exact topic.

Consider this chapter my official answer to aforementioned email truckloads. Allow my Quickie Persuasion Boosters to amplify the persuasion in your writing without any extra effort required on your part!

Ready to take your words and pump them up with rocket-fueled persuasion?

Of course you are, you smart cookie, you!

9 Quickie Boosters for Irresistible Persuasive Copy

QUICKIE BOOSTER #1 REPEAT YOURSELF

Repeat, repeat, repeat.

See what I did there? Now you'll remember this Quickie Booster!

Repetition sends your buyer's mind into a trance-like state that allows you to hold their attention. Because if you say something a lot more than once, it must be damn important!

Therapists do this all the time in their work as do professional stage magicians.

Repetition in your message is the key to creating an irresistible magnetic draw to what you have to say.

But there's an even better reason to work repetition into your copy:

People HATE being sold to.

They really, really do hate it (You know this and so do I).

Even if what you're selling is something they really want and need...

Even if they're currently miserable and have dark clouds over their heads but your service or product is going to make the sun shine again...

Even if the flood waters are rising up to their eyeballs and you're selling them the only boat in sight...

People hate being sold to.

The moment you bring "selling" into the conversation with a potential client or in a piece of copy, you trigger alarm bells that start blaring in people's heads.

But when you include repetition in your message...things start to change.

You'll draw them in. You'll inspire them. You'll motivate them.

I just did it with the previous 3 sentences!

Here's a more direct sales example from the sales page of my program *Email Persuasion Sequence*.

Notice how I describe the importance of using persuasion in your marketing emails using repetition:

"That's what makes people open every single email you send them.

"That's what makes them eagerly look forward to your name in their inbox.

"That's what makes them devour every single word like a freshly baked chocolate chip cookies right out of the oven.

"That's what makes them do what you ask them to do at the finish line."

That's the magic of repetition at work — you see yourself as part of the story being told. The promised results are just too good to pass up!

If you're not familiar with this style of writing – AKA the Quickie Booster known as Repetition – you might think this is absolutely overdone.

It's not. I promise you (remember the sold out launch for *Email Persuasion Sequence* I told you about earlier?).

Repetition in your copy magnetizes potential customers so they feel compelled to keep reading — and possibly buy your product or service on the spot!

QUICKIE BOOSTER #2
MAP OUT A DETOUR

If there's one thing in short supply these days, it's human attention.

A recent study of human behavior and memory revealed that we humans have an attention span that lasts about 8 seconds.

8...seconds...

That's shorter than the 9 second attention span of a goldfish!

A goldfish, people!

This means you and I have a tall order — work hard to keep people's minds focused on our message long enough to be persuaded and decide to buy.

Yes, this is hard — hard, but not super hard.

Because I have found a secret to keeping buyers reading (or watching):

Detours.

Detours are sharp changes in your copy or script that keep people engaged and interested as they follow your train of thought over, under and around the digital landscape.

"What's going to happen next?" is the resulting thought in your buyers' minds (remember the Curiosity Switch?).

Let's review the 3 types of Detours you can cleverly insert into your copy and video scripts, starting with…

The Topic Detour

This is the sharpest change you can introduce to a reader (or viewer).

Also known as "going down the rabbit hole", this Detour uses multiple topic changes to keep following you and your message, wondering where you'll finally end up.

It's as simple as this:

Begin your copy or video on one topic, then immediately switch to another topic before you finished the first one, " "*Every time I think about <Topic 1>, I can't help but start to think about <Topic 2>...*"

Then you wander off down the path of Topic 2 and tell *that* story.

But you're actually not wandering off at all — you're simply keeping an open loop for Topic 1 to close...eventually.

Your readers, because they're humans and not robots, will have a natural curiosity around Topic 1 (and what else you have to say about it).

In the world of storytelling and filmmaking, this is called a Cliffhanger.

Because you opened a "curiosity gap", people will stick around until you come back to Topic 1 and close that gap.

To maximize the effectiveness of The Topic Detour, keep both Topic 1 and Topic 2 relevant to your potential buyers and what they care about (i.e. don't go off on a tangent about your dog's fleas if you are going to sell your cat paintings).

Follow this little rule, and you'll get 2 messages for the price of 1 in front of your readers!

172

The Story Detour

Story — a powerful, powerful tool in your persuasion tool kit.

I've said it before in this book, but it's so important that I'll say it again...

It's human nature to want to watch, read and listen to stories.

When you inject stories into your writing, you are "hooking" your audience with the most tantalizingly tasty bait known to humans.

If you're writing an email to your subscribers, you can take The Story Detour with a sentence opener like this, *"You won't believe the news that I have for you today! But before I get into that, let me tell you this little story..."*

Yes, it's that simple.

Too simple to work?

No, just simple enough.

If you treat the human brain like an electrical circuit for your persuasive advantage, you'll see proof in the form of higher open rates, more replies to your emails and a spike in sales unlike anything you've seen pre-*Mass Persuasion Method*.

The Evidence Detour

The essence of this Detour is you making the case for why your product or service is better than anyone else's.

The Evidence Detour is ideal for sales pages (and sales videos).

Here's an example of this Detour in action, *"You'll find that this method will end your sleepless nights once and for all. But before I go into the details, here's what past customers have to say…"*

You catch that? The copy just interrupted itself!

While you're in the middle of telling your potential customer how amazing your product or service is, wander off to prove it by sharing what everyone else is already saying.

This Detour builds confidence in your offer — confidence that keeps the potential customer reading, believing and reaching for their credit card.

THE PROOF IS IN THE PERSUASION:

Rachel Cohen Olsen
13 hrs · San Diego, CA, United States

Thank you Bushra Azhar! I just soft launched my Business Celebrity course today to my list and the first person to buy my higher end offering said "Great copy! I'm in." 😊 I really needed a program like yours. Perfect timing!

QUICKIE BOOSTER #3 IT HAS TO BE YOU…

If I told you that 4 copywriting criminals were hiding in plain sight, would you believe me?

What if I *showed* you the culprits and their crimes?

These 4 copy crooks are affectionately known as:

- I
- Me
- We
- Us

They're short words. But if you let them run loose on a sales page, they will ruin your chances of ever making a sale.

So, if you scan your sales page, optin page or other pages and see these 4 criminals having a heyday, it's time to clean up your act.

Always write with your potential customer in mind. It is NEVER about you — especially in the online realm where you are deprived of benefiting from two-way conversations.

One more time:

It is NEVER about you!

Not even if you're the best in your industry.

Not even if you're a genius and can prove it.

Not even if you're an honest-to-goodness legend (or hold celebrity status).

The star of the show (AKA your business) is always "you" — not "me" or "we".

Now for an example to clarify my point:

Let's say you're the best wedding cake baker in town. You've been at it for 25 years and have thousands of photos of your creations posted online as proof of your creative genius.

Instead of writing, "I've been baking wedding cakes for 25 years," on your sales page…

You can take advantage of Quickie Booster #3 and reframe your experience with something like, "How would YOU like the expertise and experience of someone who's been creating wedding cakes for 25 years to bake a masterpiece for YOUR special day?"

Two "you's" and not a single "we", "me", "I" or "us" — good work, example cake baker!

Like the wedding cake baker with her 25 years' experience, follow a proven recipe – the Quickie Persuasion Boosters – and your potential customers will realize that what you are selling really IS for them.

Because you speak to them with your words...*directly* to them.

And all it took was getting those 4 criminals out of your copy!

QUICKIE BOOSTER #4
FORMAT LIKE THERE'S NO TOMORROW

This is probably the easiest way to level up the persuasiveness of anything you write...

Yet the fact nobody talks about it makes me want to tear my hair out.

Here's the thing:

Nobody likes to face a wall of text when they're reading something online.

Nobody.

In fact, these dreaded walls of text on your website, your emails and your social media posts have been proven to tire readers' eyes faster than reading a physical printed book.

If you have rows and rows of sentences staring at your reader, you no longer have a reader.

Because they've already escaped to do something less straining and more entertaining like watching YouTube videos of cats playing in the kitchen sink.

If you don't want an army of half blind, mega-pissed potential customers on your hands, check your formatting and break up chunks of text into manageable 1-2 sentence paragraphs.

Use the following tips and tricks to start implementing this Quickie Booster:

- Create section headings
- Bold your text
- Italicize your text
- Add a P.S. (or two) to emails
- Use different colors

These five tips and tricks – when you implement them – will make each sentence of copy jump off the page…and actually get read by potential customers (not skimmed or skipped).

Your precisely formatted text will let your words speak to your buyers' hearts and minds — because a sales page can only sell what you're offering if people read what you have to say!

QUICKIE BOOSTER #5
HOW TO TURN EVERY NO INTO A YES

In his sales strategy books, Daniel Pink explains that we can arrive at win-win situations for our customers by using a subtle trick.

Instead of saying, "But…" when you want to counter an argument, say, "Yes, *and*…"

Here's my take on this idea:

Before

Client: "This is too expensive."

You: "But that's how much such services cost!"

After

Client: "This is too expensive."

You: "Yes, and that is exactly why I am confident this will get you the results you are looking for."

Before

Client: "I don't have the money."

You: "..."

After

Client: "I don't have the money."

You: "Yes, and that is why we offer a payment plan because we really want you to succeed."

QUICKIE BOOSTER #6
THE DISRUPT THEN REFRAME (DTR)

Researchers tested the DTR technique by selling note cards for a local charity. They positioned the offer for the cards in these two ways:

- *$3 for 8 cards*
- *300 pennies for 8 cards – which is a bargain!*

Can you guess which sold better?

You're right if you guessed the second one. In fact, the second offer sold twice as many cards as the first. But why? Because of the Disrupt Then Reframe technique.

Here's how it works.

First, disrupt your potential customer's routine thought process. In the case of this study, researchers disrupted dollars by using pennies instead.

Second, while your potential customer's brain is processing this disruption, out comes the reframe! Your buyer will have less resistance to the reframe because their brain is otherwise occupied by the initial disruption.

QUICKIE BOOSTER #7
HOW TO OVERCOME BUYER'S REMORSE

The battle to close a sale doesn't end when they buy. It only takes a new form.

Customers need support to rationalize the purchase to overcome any risks of experiencing buyer's remorse.

Here are 4 mini Boosters to keep yourself off the highway to Refund City:

1. Get buyers into a community and make them visible. Hard for people to leave once they have publicly become a part of a community!

2. Encourage buyers to use a "badge" or hashtag that publicly shows that they are part of the program – again, *public accountability!*

3. As soon as they buy, get them to respond to your welcome email with one goal they want to achieve after being a part of the program. Follow up after a week, asking how they feel about their progress towards achieving it.

4. Send a personal thank you email with positive reinforcement such as, "Congratulations for investing in yourself!", "Here's how others like you have changed their lives with this program..." and "Here are 5 ways you are way ahead of the curve when it comes to..."

QUICKIE BOOSTER #8
A PSYCHOLOGY-BACKED BULLETPROOF FORMULA TO WRITE BULLETS

Time to make people stop scrolling and start drooling!

And yes, this actually *is* a formula. But don't worry! I won't ask you to order a Calculus textbook to figure it out.

This formula allows you to give your potential buyer two reasons – simultaneously – to take action.

The one thing you can do in <some unusually short time> to improve your chances <by an impressive number>.

Example: *"The one thing that takes less than five minutes but will improve your chances of being chosen as the winning candidate by at least fifty percent..."*

Here is a different version of the example, following the same formula:

"The one thing that will double your chances of being chosen as a winning candidate – and the best part? It takes less than ten minutes to implement..."

QUICKIE BOOSTER #9
THE ART OF THE PERSUASIVE TEASE

Is it possible to use hypno-triggers and sentence clues to tease your readers and create irresistible drama in your writing?

Why would I ask such a ridiculously specific question if we both didn't already know the answer?

Of course this is possible. In fact, it's *essential*.

Because there is no bigger sin than to sell without the warm-up, to reveal without the tease or to pitch without the prime.

When you write your first (or next) Blog post, Sales page or Opt-in page, your job is to keep people reading till the end, all the while helping them pay attention to important sections and topics along the way.

The 3 types of hypno-triggers I'll give you correspond to where on your page they will appear, acting as clues to tug the reader ever further down the page.

Feel free to borrow as many of these as you wish.

Openings

- *As you start reading these first few lines you will find yourself **<insert emotion you want them to feel>***

- *As you curl up on your sofa reading this email, you may start to feel* **<insert emotion you want them to feel>**
- *When you read this email to the very end you will be struck by this wave of* **<insert emotion you want them to feel>**
- *Next up, by the time you finish reading this email, you will be* **<insert emotion you want them to feel>**
- *By clicking this link, you will become* **<insert emotion you want them to feel>**
- *You don't realize it yet, but in the next four minutes you will be…*
- *It takes three minutes to read this email. This will be the best three minutes you will spend reading anything today.*
- *As every syllable of this blog post embeds itself in your brain…*

Halfway

- *Are you beginning to see how a certain thing* **<insert thing>**
- *Have you noticed* **<insert what you want them to notice>**
- *Do you remember how in second paragraph, I talked about* **<insert what you talked about>**
- *As you keep skimming through this article, you're beginning to think* **<insert what you want them to think>**
- *Read this article in its entirety, that alone will radically transform* **<insert what it will transform>**

Closings

- *As we come to the end, think about **<insert what you want them to think>***
- *As this page ends, imagine **<insert life after picture>***
- *As I wrap up this email I want you to take a moment and think really hard about **<insert what they are losing by not listening to you>***
- *Your doubt and fear about your **<insert topic>** is slipping as you finish reading this, right?*
- *If you do nothing else today as you read this email, at least do this **<insert thing you want them to do>***
- *Just one last super important part as you come to the end of this page or this video **<insert super important thing>***
- *One last thing as we come to the end **<insert what you want them to think>***

****

That's all folks!

Or is it?

Yes, we have arrived at the end of the book. But your journey to mastery of the *Mass Persuasion Method* and all it components, techniques and formulas has only begun.

I hope you've found my musings to be insightful, fun and most of all helpful for bringing in more sales that you ever thought possible.

THE PROOF IS IN THE PERSUASION:

Carolin Weber Soldo
4 mins · Buffalo, NY, United States

Yes, I'm one of Bushra's Graduates and after taking her course, I was able to BEAT my highest income month in January 2015 and yet again almost sell out Brand Your Passions, my 4 Month Mastermind Program for new Coaches.

Small businesses can score the BIG bucks — I've seen it happen again and again.

My business was so tiny you couldn't have picked it out with a microscope!

But persuasion changed the game for me.

And it's changed the game for the thousands of other small business owners who have joined me in this our Persuasion Revolution.

The game can change for you too, my darling buttercup.

So now, I hand the baton off to you — you understand the principles of persuasion and the time to take action is here.

Apply what you read. Apply what you learned.

And apply it all consistently.

That's when you'll see growth and expansion…

In your business, in your fan base…

And in your self-confidence and faith in your ability to make those BIG dreams come true.

Now go forth and conquer, my darling buttercup!

When you do, please remember to drop me a line.

I'll be here waiting with your celebratory Nutella-covered croissant!

Nutella-Covered Nuggets of Wisdom

- Words are the life force of your business. The only chance you have of "making it" in business is to use the right words in the right way.
- Keep the 4 copywriting criminals – I, Me, Us, We – far away from everything you write in order to maximize the persuasive powers of your copy.
- The 4 Quickie Boosters that keep readers reading long enough to actually become buyers are Repetition, Detours, Writing to Your Reader and Formatting.

WHAT'S NEXT

WANT TO GO DEEPER, PERSUADE FASTER AND SELL MORE?

I got ya covered!

The Persuasion Revolution is the only place on the Internet that makes Persuasion sexy, classy…and fun!

How you ask, my darling?

Aside from new (and free) Persuasion Hooks at www. ThePersuasionRevolution.com that you can use right away on your clients, prospects or spouses…

There is a cohort of tantalizing offers awaiting those of you who are ready for your *own* Persuasion Revolution!

THE PROOF IS IN THE PERSUASION:

 **L'Erin Alta**
1 hr

I look forward to Bushra's offerings with the same level of ravenous enthusiasm that my mini-poodle uses when devouring her snatch.

Sometimes, when I'm going through EPS 1.0 or MPM or The Persuasion Hacks Lab material, I become so flooded with unyielding gratitude and love for our fearless leader, that I have to tell somebody! (And here we are...)

I have learned SO much from her -- not only because of her insatiably generous offerings that consistently go FAR above and beyond what she promises, but because she's SO. DAMN. GOOD. my business has become an unrecognizable powerhouse as a result of working with her!

I consider myself honored, privileged and very, very blessed to have found her corner of the virtual world. A million bows of gratitude, Bushra!

-- Does anyone else feel the same way about our beloved?

MASS PERSUASION METHOD

Master the 8 psychological Persuasion Switches to sell without the sleaze, persuade without the ick and convert without the lies.

Want to win hearts, minds and wallets using the Psychology of Persuasion? Get front row tickets when this show opens up again:

www.MassPersuasionMethod.com

THE PERSUASION HACKS LAB

The Persuasion Hacks Lab is the largest collection of persuasion hacks, word for word scripts and psychological tactics on Planet Internet.

The PH Lab opens for 48 Hours every month. Reserve your spot on the waiting list to be notified when it opens: www.PersuasionHacksLab.com

THE EMAIL PERSUASION SEQUENCE 3.0

The world's first licensed-based system that gives you scripts, templates and swipe files for every single email you will ever need to send to your list.

With EPS 3.0, you just swipe, hit send and cha-ching!
Be the first to find out when licenses are available again:
www.EmailPersuasionSequence.com

THE PROOF IS IN THE PERSUASION:

Maureen Witten ▸ 60 Second Persuasion
2 hrs · Centennial, CO, United States ·

I just wanted to say that I started January pretty damn low. I had a 20% or lower email open rate, I couldn't pay people to get on my list and my launch completely flopped at the end of December. My FB ads were shit too.

I decided to use January to finally make time to really use my trainings that I'd purchased from Bushra- and I've got all of them! 😊 I had listened to them before, but never really applied the steps or took real action.

It's feb 3rd, and by applying the action suggested in Bushra's FB Ads training in the Lab, the Landing page training in MPM and the Opt-in training in the Lab, blog training in the Lab, and the welcome email sequence in EPS, I've got two ads converting at 6 cents per click, a blog post that's gotten over 400 clicks and tons of shares, 13 new subscribers in 24 hours time (I have a small list, so this is huge), and the open AND click rate on my email welcome sequence is above 50%!

That may be small potatoes for some, but it's a huge leap forward for me. I plan on using the webinar training in MPM and the webinar email sequence in EPS for a (hopefully) successful launch next month! Thank you Bushra- my faith in my business is restored in because of your trainings!

SOLD OUT LAUNCH

Use buyer psychology to create, launch and sell out your online product in 35 days without losing your sanity, your dignity or your belief in human decency.

Get on the VIP List to claim a front row seat when SOL reopens: www.SoldOutLaunch.com

THE PERSUASION SHOW WITH BUSHRA AZHAR

Hack your way to rebuttal-proof arguments, dismissal-proof emails and back button-proof websites.

Enjoy the best episodes of the podcast – and get instant easy access to the full transcripts and worksheets – at www.ThePersuasionShow.com

60 SECOND PERSUASION

All aboard tiny business owners (less than 300k in revenue)! This is the place where you will find bite-sized actionable tips on using psychology of persuasion in your business...everything from website copy, design, emails, client communication, negotiations, positioning — the whole ninety-nine yards!

Stop the bullshit. Take the oath. Join our free community: www.Facebook.com/Groups/60SecondPersuasion

ABOUT BUSHRA AZHAR

THE UNVARNISHED, UNEMBELLISHED, HONEST-TO-GOODNESS-OR-I'LL-TURN-INTO-A-TOAD-WITH-WARTS, TRUTH ABOUT MYSELF

I am a Persuasion Strategist, and I teach tiny businesses how to make big bucks using the Psychology of Persuasion.

I've been featured in Forbes, Fast Company and other great places on the internet. I've worked with big a$$ companies like Pepsi and Unilever as a (overpaid – but don't tell anyone!) consultant.

That's the short version. Here's the longer version…

When I started out in the online business 2 ½ years ago, I had no freaking clue what I was doing.

No clue.

At all.

My family and friends didn't even know I was doing anything online.

There I was hosting webinars, writing emails and selling programs — they were none the wiser.

I only told them about what I was doing after I had reached a measure of success I found to be worth talking about.

Yep, I'm weird like that!

Since then, I've enjoyed some pretty cool successes like:

- Making $32K and working with 615 clients all in a span of my first 5 months in business with zero online connections

- Getting my first sale ($799 done-for-you package) without a sales page because my website About Page was so compelling

- Running a now 7 figure business I created from absolutely nothing. It started to grow in under 3 months and hasn't stopped!

I've also attracted scores of haters and copycats...

But even more friends. Oh, my friends...

I've met so many amazing people because of my business – both online and off – it blows my mind.

They live around the world, and I can't tell you how much I adore them all.

My business has been my source of panic (when there's a launch and the darn hosting company dies on me!), my fulfillment and my deep, deep joy.

I have laughed and I have cried and I have screamed.

I have had sleepless nights and nights when I was half asleep while hosting a webinar.

I started it all on a wing and a prayer.

Wondering what "this online thing" was all about...

I didn't have a team (unless you count my 6-year-old playing with Canva).

I didn't have an office (thank heavens for giant closets).

I didn't have a fancy computer (the only Mac in my life was a Big Mac).

I didn't have an accountant (heck I AM the trained accountant in this joint but lost touch with my debits and credits over the past few years).

I have zero design sense (just take a look at older versions of my website, but wear a pair of shades first – don't say I didn't warn you!).

I shot sales videos like selfies (yep you guessed it...no tripod).

I didn't have a VA...

Or a tech team...

Or an business coach.

I am a one woman army...

I am just a mom....

I learn new things, try stuff and fail...

Again and again and again...

I say "f-it" more than "got it!"

I work through nap times and I try to hustle.

But it's hard when you have mouths to feed, brains to grow and two short and extremely loud people to entertain.

And you know what?

It's OK…

It's okay to work hard…

To try every trick in the book…

I put my heart, soul and money into my business…

I did it over and over again before I began to see returns.

I tried and failed and tried and failed…

And then finally, I succeeded.

Kinda like a toddler learning to walk…they start out looking like a drunk adult tripping over things, stumbling head-first into tables and then…one day…they start walking…just like that!

I managed to build a million-dollar business, an email list of 23,000 and a buyer list of 4,000 in less than 2 years.

Particularly proud I am of the fact that almost 20% of my list is made up of buyers (compared to the typical 4% to 5%).

I also have crazy-high conversion numbers. My email open rates are as high as 80% and my Facebook ad conversions are as low as 20 cents.

But I know that while all this is wonderful, while I feel great gratitude…

This is not the end of the story.

You can bet your life, and mine, on that!

I know I will try again and fail again.

But that's what this journey is all about…

Being true to who you are…

Building a business that you believe in.

This is the beautiful, unglamorous, deeply satisfying reality of a multitasking mumpreneur.

I feel lucky and blessed to be able to play…

And I wouldn't change it for the world!

If you'd like to know more, check out my online home at www.ThePersuasionRevolution.com

Made in the USA
Las Vegas, NV
15 January 2024

84411298R00109